Jelly Yarn

20 Cool Projects
for girls to Knit and Crochet

Kathleen Greco and Nick Greco

kp krause publications
Cincinnati, OH

mycraftivity.com
Connect. Create. Explore.

and Dimensional Illustrators, Inc.
P.O. Box 543, Southampton, PA 18966, jellyyarns.com
Jelly Yarn™ is a trademark of Kathleen Greco/Dimensional Illustrators, Inc. All rights Reserved.

Other fine Krause Publications titles are available from your local bookstore, craft supply store, online retailer or visit our website at www.fwpublications.com.

12 11 10 09 08   5 4 3 2 1

Distributed in Canada by Fraser Direct
100 Armstrong Avenue
Georgetown, ON, Canada L7G 5S4
Tel: (905) 877-4411

Distributed in the U.K. and Europe by David & Charles
Brunel House, Newton Abbot, Devon, TQ12 4PU, England
Tel: (+44) 1626 323200, Fax: (+44) 1626 323319
Email: postmaster@davidandcharles.co.uk

Distributed in Australia by Capricorn Link
P.O. Box 704, S. Windsor NSW, 2756 Australia
Tel: (02) 4577-3555

F+W PUBLICATIONS, INC.

Library of Congress Cataloging-in-Publication Data

Greco, Kathleen.
  Jelly yarn : 20 cool projects for girls to knit and crochet / Kathleen Greco and Nick Greco.
      p. cm.
  Includes index.
  ISBN-13: 978-0-89689-803-5 (pbk. : alk. paper)
  ISBN-10: 0-89689-803-2 (pbk. : alk. paper)
  1. Knitting--Patterns. 2. Crocheting--Patterns. 3. Vinyl fibers. I. Greco, Nick. II. Title.
  TT820.G8242 2008
  746.43'2041--dc22
                        2008033746

Metric Conversion Chart		
To convert	**to**	**Multiply by**
Inches	Centimeters	2.54
Centimeters	Inches	0.4
Feet	Centimeters	30.5
Centimeters	Feet	0.03
Yards	Meters	0.9
Meters	Yards	1.1

Printed in China

For Mom and Dad
Thank you for your creative inspiration!

Acknowledgments

We would like to extend our thanks to everyone who has worked creatively with Jelly Yarn. Special thanks to Deborah Davis for her playful, innovative book design. Thank you to Jay Staten of F+W Publications, for her creative guidance and expertise. Our deep appreciation to our talented models Madalyn, Magdelina, Olivia, and Pryanka for their professionalism while modeling the projects in this book. We also wish to extend our appreciation to Vashti for her designs and, for loving Jelly Yarn as much as we do. Many thanks to Carrie and Judy for their creative designs. Our sincere gratitude to our talented photographer Joe VanDeHatert, for his brilliant photos, and to Wendy for her hair and makeup styling. Thank you to Jo Anne Yamamoto, owner of Mimi and Maggie, for their selection of spirited girls clothing. Love to all our friends and family.

–Nick and Kathleen Greco

Credits

Creative Director **Kathleen Greco** *Dimensional Illustrators, Inc. / Jelly Yarns*

Executive Editor **Nick Greco** *Dimensional Illustrators, Inc. / Jelly Yarns*

Design and Typography **Deborah Davis** *Deborah Davis Design*

Knit and Crochet Designer **Kathleen Greco**

Contributing Designers

Flying Jelly Ring page 62 **Vashti Braha**

Sports Bottle Sling page 74 **Vashti Braha**

Jellyfish Purse page 90 **Vashti Braha**

Jump Rope page 28 **Judy Patkos**

Hair Accessories page 66 **Carrie A. Sullivan**

Fashion Photographer **Joe VanDeHatert V Studio**

Knit and Crochet Techniques, and Project Photography
Kathleen Greco *Dimensional Illustrators, Inc. / Jelly Yarns*

Crochet Pattern Editor **Randy Cavaliere**

Knit Pattern Editor **Amy Polcyn**

Hair and Makeup Stylist **Wendy VanDeHatert**

Schematic Illustrator **Deborah Davis** *Deborah Davis Design*

4 How to Knit 100

5 How to Crochet 108

6 Important Stuff 116

1

Introduction
All About Jelly Yarn

You are about to begin an amazing adventure into the fun-filled world of Jelly Yarn. Jelly Yarn is a new, colorful yarn that is ideal for knitting and crocheting one-of-kind purses and accessories. This unique yarn gives you the ability to create cool, glossy textures that are impossible to create with traditional fiber yarns. The 100% vinyl yarn is strong, flexible, and completely waterproof. We had so much fun developing Jelly Yarn that we decided to name

all the colors after our favorite candies and ices with cool, fun names like Hot Pink Candy, Blue Taffy, Black Licorice, Lemon-Lime Ice, Raspberry Sorbet, and Pink Peppermint Glow, just to name a few. We're sure you'll have lots of fun with your girlfriends knitting and crocheting each yummy project in *Jelly Yarn: 20 Cool Projects for Girls to Knit and Crochet*, designed especially for you.

All About Jelly Yarn

Jelly Yarn! What is it?

Jelly Yarn is a new, round and glossy yarn, that's ideal for knitting or crocheting. It's made of 100 percent vinyl, and comes in 14 yummy colors. The yarn is simple to work because the stitches are easy to see, and they won't split like some fiber yarns. Jelly Yarn works great on metal needles and hooks, (more on that, later). Chapters 2 and 3 are filled with 20 fantastic knit and crochet projects. Chapters 4 and 5 teach you how to knit and crochet, and will help you sharpen your skills and build your confidence. Chapter 6 includes important stuff about assembling your projects, plus Skill Level and Stitch Pattern Guides. To help you find the materials used in each project, don't forget to check the Resources on page 126. Sure, it's nice to knit or crochet wool hats and scarves, but how cool is "glossy" waterproof yarn! You can make purses, jewelry, belts, jewelry boxes, and other cool stuff to enjoy all year round. Have a fun-tastic time!

Knitting with Jelly Yarn

• Begin knitting colorful Jelly Bracelets, an Ankle Bracelet, and a Jelly Necklace with matching pendant, page 16. They're easy to knit with a simple I-cord technique.

• Keep your secrets in the dark by knitting your own Green Peppermint Glow-in-the-dark Diary Cover, page 20.

• Make something for your best pet pal! The Pet Collar and Leash, page 24, is safe, glow-in-the-dark nighttime fun.

• For hours of fun with your friends, you'll love knitting the cool, Pink and Green Glow-in-the-dark I-cord Jump Rope, page 28.

• Another I-cord project, the Fun Belt, page 32, combines Blue Taffy and Lemon-Lime Ice colors, to match your outfits.

• You'll be the hit of the party with a unique Raspberry Sorbet Feather Party Purse, page 36, created in a simple knit stitch. The feather boa handle is so cool!

• The easy-to-knit Jewelry Box, page 40, uses five Honey Gold Jelly Yarn squares. It's a one-of-a-kind jewel box for your most prized gems.

• Small and cute, the Mini Purse, page 44, is knit with Lemon-Lime Ice and Blue Taffy colors. It's perfect for carrying your important things.

• The summer fun Beach Bag, page 48, is knit in the round, and combines waterproof Lemon-Lime Ice, with Hot Pink Candy Jelly Yarn stripes.

• The Knapsack, page 52, uses garter and stockinette stitch patterns while mixing the Raspberry Sorbet Jelly Yarn with an acrylic fiber yarn to create a unique tote bag that's sturdy, attractive, and fun to carry.

Crocheting with Jelly Yarn

• Begin with a cool Glow Belt, page 58, made with single crochet using Pink Peppermint Glow Jelly Yarn.

• You and your friends will enjoy tossing around our fabulous Flying Jelly Ring, page 62, featuring Blue Smoothie Jelly Yarn trimmed in Pink Parfait. Add jingle bells, and create a unique musical Tambourine, page 65.

• The fun Hair Accessories, page 66, include Beaded Clip and Flower Clasp Barrettes with Raspberry Sorbet, Hot Pink Candy, and Lemon-Lime Ice Jelly Yarn. For special occasions, make the beaded Silver Icing Tiara. It's an easy project to crochet, and it's great fun to wear.

• You don't have to worry about the rain anymore! Our water-resistant Lemon-Lime Ice Jelly Boot Sleeves, page 70, are the perfect solution for those rainy days. Crochet in easy single and double crochet, and add large flower buttons.

• Have fun playing sports while using your own Sport Bottle Sling, page 74. It's quick and easy to crochet in the round with Blue Taffy Jelly Yarn.

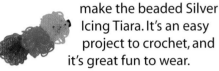

• You can never have enough bracelets. Create stretchy cool Ice Jelly Bracelets and a Jelly Bangle, page 78.

• Ever see a crochet flower in a snow globe? Now it's possible with waterproof Jelly Yarn. Crochet flowers in the round, for a make-it-yourself Snow Globe, page 82. Use Pink, and Green Glow-in-the-dark, Jelly Yarn and you'll have fun making these cool glowing globes!

• The crochet Amigurumi Starfish, page 86, is a Jelly Yarn toy that gets its inspiration from Japan. We used fine Blue Smoothie Jelly Yarn, worked in the round to create this adorably friendly pal, that's sure to get a lot of attention.

• Discover a new use for an old CD as the bottom support for this unique Jellyfish Purse, page 90, with Pink Peppermint glow-in-the-dark Jelly Yarn. It's easy to crochet with single and double crochet stitches in the round.

• Crochet the Fun Pack, page 94, with Blue Smoothie Jelly Yarn using single and double crochet stitches. The bag features a sturdy shoulder strap and heavy-duty zipper that holds everything, yet weighs nothing. Add an attractive butterfly pin, and you're ready to go!

Now that you have learned all about the cool projects you can create with Jelly Yarn, it's time to start your knitting and crocheting adventure!

Jelly Yarn Colors

Jelly Yarn has four different color categories. Here's a sampling of the 14 glossy colors Fine and Bulky. You can substitute any color in the patterns as long as it is the same weight. The colorful yarns are named after our favorite yummy foods but unfortunately they're not edible.

Translucent Jelly Yarn

These four cool translucent colors let light pass through with a yummy effect. The shiny colors remind us of seashore candy and cool ices.

Blue Taffy

Looking at Blue Taffy Jelly Yarn is like floating in a warm pool of blue water. The shiny translucent quality of this yarn is rich and fun. Blue Taffy yarn is used for the Fun Belt, Mini Purse, and Sports Bottle Sling.

Lemon-Lime Ice

You'll think of summer lemon ice every time you use this refreshing Lemon-Lime Ice Jelly Yarn. This cool translucent yarn glows neon under black light. Lemon-Lime Ice appears in the Jelly Jewelry, Mini Purse, Beach Bag, Hair Accessories, and Jelly Boot Sleeves.

Hot Pink Candy

This delicious-looking yarn, is perfect for summer fun! The hot translucent yarn has a warm neon glow under black light. Hot Pink Candy is featured in the Jelly Jewelry, Beach Bag, and Hair Accessories

Raspberry Sorbet

The amazing purple transparency of Raspberry Sorbet is like looking through a glass of grape juice. The Raspberry Parfait appears in the Jelly Jewelry, Feather Party Purse, Knapsack, Hair Accessories, and Jelly Bracelets.

Opaque Jelly Yarn

These four solid yarn colors produce hip glossy textures that are ideal for any project. They are named after our favorite ice cream dessert, frozen blended drink, and candies.

Black Licorice

Black Licorice looks like stretchy candy strips. This yarn when knit or crocheted, has the look and feel of shiny patent leather. The opaque quality gives this yummy yarn a high glossy sheen that is great for belts and purses.

Pink Parfait

Pink Parfait Jelly Yarn is as light and bright as cotton candy. The shinny opaque color adds a girl-power to any project. Pink Parfait is featured in the Jelly Jewelry Necklace, and Flying Jelly Ring.

Wild Cherry Red

Wild Cherry Red Jelly Yarn is bright and fun. This glossy, opaque cheery yarn is bound to attract a lot of attention. The bright cherry red color is great for many projects including, jewelry and purses.

Blue Smoothie

The deep azure Blue Smoothie Jelly Yarn resembles a creamy thick, frosty drink. The solid opaque quality of this yarn adds a smooth look for any outdoor project. Blue Smoothie is used to create the Flying Jelly Ring, Jelly Amigurumi Starfish, and Fun Pack.

Metallic and Clear Jelly Yarn

Three unique yarns add sparkle, glitter and shine to any project. The yarns are named after sugary sweets we enjoy including pancake syrup, and cookie icing.

Ice

Ice Jelly Yarn is a completely transparent yarn. When held up to light, the clear Ice texture looks like you're gazing into a sparkling diamond. The glossy Jelly Bracelets are crocheted with Ice Jelly Yarn.

Honey Gold

Glistening Honey Gold Jelly Yarn is a clear strand of yarn that's sprinkled with gold glitter. This gold-speckled yarn creates a shimmery texture. The Jewelry Box project is knit with Honey Gold Jelly Yarn.

Silver Icing

The shiny Silver Icing Jelly Yarn is a clear strand that's dotted with silver glitter. This sparkling yarn resembles glistening snow. Silver Ice Jelly Yarn is featured in the Glow Diary Cover, Hair Accessories, and Tambourine.

Glow-in-the-Dark Jelly Yarn

These three magically optic yarns glow-in-the-dark. After exposure to natural or indoor light, the yarn glows in total darkness. The longer the exposure to light, the longer the yarn will glow. The glow colors are named after our favorite mint candy.

Pink Peppermint Glow

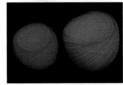

Pink Peppermint Glow Jelly Yarn has a fresh pink color. After exposure to light, this yarn has a wonderful pink afterglow in the absence of light. Pink Peppermint Glow is used in the Jump Rope, Glow Belt, Snow Globe Flower, and Jellyfish Purse.

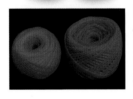

Green Peppermint Glow

The Green Peppermint Glow Jelly Yarn is the perfect color for many fun projects. After exposure to light, Green Peppermint Glow emits a green glow. The Green Peppermint Glow is featured in the Glow Diary Cover, Pet Collar and Leash, Jump Rope, Fun Belt, and Snow Globe Flower.

Vanilla Peppermint Glow

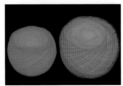

Vanilla Peppermint Glow Jelly Yarn has a soft, creamy texture. The lack of color makes this the brightest glowing yarn, compared to Green Peppermint and Pink Peppermint. After exposure to light, Vanilla Peppermint Glow emits a bright green glow.

Important Stuff About Jelly Yarn

Jelly Yarn is a round, glossy vinyl yarn that is available in two weights: Fine and Bulky. Both weights can be used for either knitting or crocheting. In this book, several crochet patterns are designed using Fine, because the strands bend easily on the hook. Some knit patterns are designed with Bulky due to the stronger texture of the yarn. Follow the yarn ball specifications for using Fine or Bulky in the pattern.

Fine Jelly Yarn

Thin and flexible, Fine Jelly Yarn is similar in thickness to a sport weight (4-ply yarn), great for either knitting or crocheting. The Fine weight is used on projects that are particularly small and flexible using US 8/5mm size needles, or US I/5.5mm hooks or smaller. The following knit patterns use Fine Jelly Yarn: Jelly Jewelry Ankle Bracelet, Glow Diary Cover, Pet Collar and Leash, Jewelry Box, and Mini Purse. For crochet, these patterns use Fine Jelly Yarn: Glow Belt, Hair Accessories, Jelly Boot Sleeves, Sports Bottle Sling, Jelly Bracelets, Snow Globe Flower, Jelly Amigurumi Starfish, Jellyfish Purse, and Fun Pack.

Bulky Jelly Yarn

Thick and fun, Bulky Jelly Yarn is similar in thickness to a worsted weight (double yarn), it works up quickly for both knitting or crocheting. Larger needles and hooks create a slick, sturdy texture. Bulky Jelly Yarn works best with size US 8/5mm needles or larger. These are the knit patterns with Bulky Jelly Yarn: Jelly Jewelry Bracelets, Jump Rope, Fun Belt, Feather Party Purse, and Beach Bag. For crocheting, size J/6mm or larger works best with Bulky Jelly Yarn. These crochet patterns use Bulky Jelly Yarn: Flying Jelly Ring, and Tamborine.

Knitting Needles and Crochet Hooks

With either Fine or Bulky weight Jelly Yarn, we recommend knitting or crocheting with metal hooks or needles. Any metal brand will work, but Susan Bates® Silvalume® metal needles or hooks work well because of their smooth satin surface.

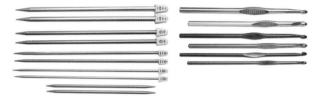

Helping Jelly Yarn Glide

Jelly Yarn is 100 percent vinyl and so much fun to use! If your tension, (how tight your stitches are), is too tight, your stitches on the needle or hook may not slide. To help make the stitches glide easily, we recommend using a little hand lotion. Lotion for dry hands works best because it is thicker, but any kid-safe hand lotion will work.

How to help the stitches glide on a knitting needle:

• *Wipe a little hand lotion along the stitches on the needle, and continue knitting.*

How to help the stitches glide on a crochet hook:

• *Wipe a little hand lotion on the hook, and continue crocheting.*

How to help the yarn glide when you knit or crochet:

• *You can also wipe a little hand lotion on the yarn strand, and continue knitting or crocheting.*

Tying Knots

Knitting or crocheting with Jelly Yarn is a little different than fiber yarn. Because of the slick surface of the vinyl yarn strand, knots are needed to prevent the stitches from unraveling. Use a double knot, (square knot), to keep secure.

How to make a double knot:

• *Place the right strand over the left strand and put the strand under the loop.*

• *Next, place the left strand over the right strand and put the strand under the loop. Pull the stands tightly to make a knot, then release.*

Make a double knot when instructed to do so in the pattern. Here are some examples when you will need to make a double knot.

• *When knitting, make a double knot after the last cast on stitch.*

• *When crocheting, make a double knot after you make a slip knot.*

• *When knitting or crocheting, make a double knot when joining yarns.*

• *When knitting or crocheting, make a double knot after you fasten off or bind off.*

Blocking Jelly Yarn

Blocking with Jelly Yarn is not like blocking with fiber yarn. If your knit or crochet piece has curled when you finish, block the piece before assembling, or as instructed in the pattern.

The best knit stitch for creating a flat texture is the Knit Through the Back Loop stitch, page 104. The best crochet stitch for a flat texture is the Single Crochet, page 112.

How to block Jelly Yarn:

• *Place the piece on a flat hard surface, like a wooden or plastic board, and make the sides even.*

• *Make sure the piece is flat and even. Using colorful duct tape, found in craft stores, tape the edges of the piece to the surface.*

• *Place a heavy weight such as a dictionary or phone book on top, and leave overnight.*

• *The next day, remove the weight and tape. Assemble as instructed in the pattern.*

2

Knit Jelly Yarn Projects

Jelly Jewelry

beginner

Now you can knit your own Jelly Jewelry! Make a basic Jelly Bracelet with bulky Lemon-Lime Ice. Then, choose colorful Raspberry Sorbet or Hot Pink Candy to create Jelly Bracelets with charms. Switch to fine Honey Gold and crochet a cute Ankle Bracelet. We used Pink Peppermint Glow to make a Jelly Necklace with a pendant. You'll love making and wearing this fun jewelry!

Needles

US 6 (4mm) and US 8 (5mm) double-pointed needles, or size needed to obtain gauge.

Gauge

Alert! For the Jelly Ankle Bracelet, make sure the charm loops slide over the I-cord. For the Jelly Necklace, make sure the larger jump ring slides over the I-cord.

Yarn

Basic Jelly Bracelet
Partial ball Bulky Jelly Yarn
Color: Lemon-Lime Ice
65yds (60m) / 240g (100% vinyl)

Heart Jelly Bracelet
Partial ball Bulky Jelly Yarn
Color: Hot Pink Candy
65yds (60m) / 240g (100% vinyl)

Butterfly and Stars Jelly Bracelet
Partial ball Bulky Jelly Yarn
Color: Raspberry Sorbet
65yds (60m) / 240g (100% vinyl)

Jelly Ankle Bracelet
Partial ball Fine Jelly Yarn
Color: Honey Gold
85yds (78m) / 200g (100% vinyl)

Jelly Necklace
Partial ball Fine Jelly Yarn
Color: Pink Peppermint Glow
85yds (78m) / 200g (100% vinyl)

Materials

10 – Jewelry clasps (2 per bracelet or necklace)

4 – Heart charms with ring (bracelet)

4 – Butterfly and star charms with ring (bracelet)

4 – Shoe charms (ankle bracelet)

½" (1cm) Jump ring (necklace)

¾" (2cm) Jump ring (necklace)

Round pendant (necklace)

2 – Mini chain nose pliers

Stitch Guide

I-Cord page 104

Finished Measurements

About 6" (15cm) long bracelet

About 7" (18cm) long ankle bracelet

About 20" (50cm) long necklace

Leftovers!

This project is great for using leftover yarn because you don't need much.

Jelly Jewelry Patterns

Basic Jelly Bracelet Pattern

With larger needles and Lemon-Lime Ice Bulky yarn, cast on 3 stitches. Leave 4" (10cm) for sewing to the clasp.

- *Tie a double knot after the last cast on stitch with the tail and yarn ball strands.*

Row 1: Without turning needle, slide stitches to the right point and knit the 3 stitches across.

- *Be careful not to slide stitches off the needle.*

Repeat Row 1 for 6" (15cm) or desired circumference for wrist.

- *Remember to pull yarn tightly after the 1st knit stitch.*

Bind off tightly. Leave 4" (10cm) for sewing to the clasp.

- *Do not block!*

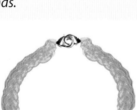

Finishing

Attaching Clasps

Thread cast on tail strand through clasp hole and tie a double knot. Repeat on bind off end.

Heart Jelly Bracelet Pattern

With larger needles and Hot Pink Candy Bulky yarn, use Basic Jelly Bracelet Pattern.

Finishing

Attaching Heart Charms

Hold the ring of the 1st charm with the pliers. With the 2nd plier, open the ring and slide it onto a stitch along the outside, exactly 1¼" (3cm) from the clasp. Close ring tightly. Attach the rest of the charms at 1¼" (3cm) intervals equally spaced around the bracelet.

Butterfly and Stars Jelly Bracelet Pattern

With larger needles and Raspberry Sorbet Bulky yarn, use Heart Jelly Bracelet Pattern. Use 2 butterfly and 2 star charms in place of the heart charms.

Jelly Ankle Bracelet Pattern

With smaller needles and Honey Gold Fine yarn, cast on 3 stitches. Leave 4" (10cm) for sewing to the clasp.

- *Tie a double knot after the last cast on stitch with the tail and yarn ball strands.*

Row 1: Without turning needle, slide stitches to the right point and knit the 3 stitches across.

- *Be careful not to slide stitches off the needle.*

Repeat Row 1 for 7" (18cm) or desired circumference for ankle.

- *Pull yarn tightly after the 1st knit stitch.*

Bind off tightly. Leave 4" (10cm) for sewing to the clasp.

- *Do not block!*

Finishing

Attaching Charms
Slide the ring charms along the I-cord, equally spaced around the bracelet.

Attaching Clasps
Use Basic Jelly Bracelet finishing.

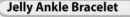

Jelly Necklace Pattern

With smaller needles and Pink Peppermint Glow Fine yarn, cast on 3 stitches. Leave 4" (10cm) for sewing to the clasp.

- *Tie a double knot after the last cast on stitch with the tail and yarn ball strands.*

Row 1: Without turning needle, slide stitches to the right point and knit the 3 stitches across.

- *Be careful not to slide stitches off the needle.*

Repeat Row 1 for 20" (50cm) or desired length.

- *Pull yarn tightly after the 1st knit stitch.*

Bind off tightly. Leave 4" (10cm) for sewing to the clasp.

- *Do not block!*

Finishing

Attaching Pendant
Hold small jump ring with the 1st plier. With the 2nd plier, twist ring open and slide pendant on ring. Close the ring. Hold large jump ring with pliers, and with the other plier twist the ring open. Slide small ring onto the large ring. Close the ring. Slide large jump ring over necklace.

Attaching Clasps
Use Basic Jelly Bracelet finishing.

Jelly Bracelets Lemon-Lime Ice, Hot Pink Candy, Raspberry Sorbet	½" (1cm)	
6" (15cm)		
Jelly Ankle Bracelet Honey Gold	¼" (.63cm)	
7" (18cm)		
Jelly Necklace Pink Peppermint Glow	¼" (.63cm)	
20" (50cm)		

Glow Diary Cover

beginner

Create your own diary from a spiral notebook, and knit a Green Peppermint Glow-in-the-dark beaded Diary Cover. Add small glow-in-the-dark pony beads with Silver Icing yarn to create a fun, glowing texture. Decorate the cover with alphabet beads and key charms. You'll have a cool place to write about your knitting fun in your new glow-in-the-dark diary!

Needles

US 10 (6mm) needles, or size needed to obtain gauge.

Gauge

15 stitches and 20 rows = 4" (10cm)

Yarn

1 ball Fine Jelly Yarn
Color: Green Peppermint Glow
85yds (78m) / 200g (100% vinyl)

1 ball Fine Jelly Yarn
Color: Silver Icing
85yds (78m) / 200g (100% vinyl)

Materials

5"x 7" (12cm x 18cm) Spiral notebook

433 – (5mm) Glow-in-the-dark pony beads

Alphabet beads

3 – Key charms

Tapestry needle

Invisible thread

Sewing needle

Strong white glue

Stitch Guide

Knit through the Back Loop page 104

Whipstitch page 118

Finished Measurements

14" wide x 7" (36cm x 18cm) high

Glow Diary Cover Pattern

Front and Back

With Green Peppermint Glow, cast on 53 stitches. Leave 6" (15cm) for sewing.

- *Tie a double knot after the last cast on stitch with the tail and yarn ball strands.*

Row 1: Knit through the back loop of each stitch across the row.

Repeat Row 1 for 2½" (6cm).

String 424 beads on Silver Icing.

Change to Silver Icing.

Next Row: Knit through the back loop of each stitch across the row.

Next Beaded Row: Slide bead up to the needle and knit through the back loop of the 1st stitch. Repeat for each stitch across the row.

Repeat last 2 rows for 2" (5cm), alternating plain and beaded rows.

Change to Green Peppermint Glow.

Repeat Row 1 for 2½" (6cm).

- *While knitting is still on the needle, compare height of knit cover against height of notebook. Make sure they are the same. If your knitting is too short, keep knitting until they are the same height.*

Bind off loosely.

Leave 6" (15cm) for sewing.

Block piece flat.

Finishing

Attaching the Alphabet Beads

Cut an 8" (20cm) piece of yarn and tie a knot 2" (5cm) from one end. String 4 glow-in-the-dark beads. Next, with the alphabet beads, string the letters M and Y. String 1 glow-in-the-dark bead. Then, string the letters D, I, A, R, and Y, followed by 4 glow-in-the-dark beads. Tie a knot after the last bead. With right side up, center beaded strand and pull ends through cover with a crochet hook. Tie a double knot with both ends.

- *Make sure the cover stays flat. If the cover is bending, the knot is too tight.*

Attaching the Key Charms

With sewing needle, thread a 12" (30cm) piece of invisible thread. Sew each charm to the cover.

- *You can use 1 piece of thread for all the charms by stringing it behind the knit piece to attach each charm.*

Sewing the Cover to the Notebook

Place knitted cover on a flat surface, with wrong side up. Place opened notebook centered on cover. The cover should overlap on both sides.

Open the notebook to the back inside cover. Fold the overlapping edge of the knitted piece over the side edge of the inside back cover to form a flap.

Thread tapestry needle with remaining yarn tail or 20" (50cm) of yarn, and sew top seam of flap, using a whipstitch. Next, work the needle through the loops along the edge from the top to the bottom. Sew the bottom seam closed with a whipstitch. Repeat for front inside cover.

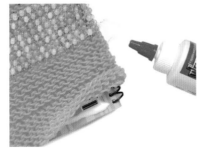

Close the diary with the back cover facing up, pull back the knit bottom edge and apply a small amount of glue along the notebook. Repeat for the top edge. Turn book over and repeat on front cover. Press firmly and apply a weight, such as a thick book, until dry.

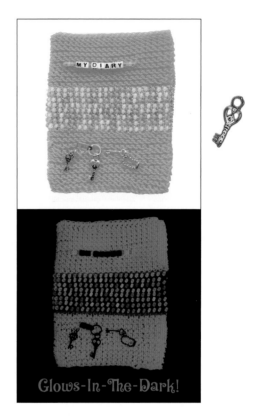

Glows-In-The-Dark!

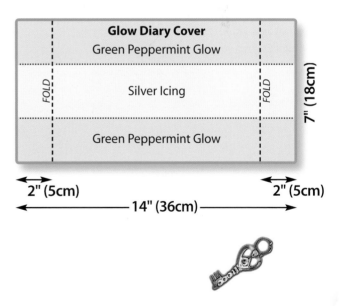

Glow Diary Cover

	Green Peppermint Glow	
FOLD	Silver Icing	FOLD
	Green Peppermint Glow	

7" (18cm)

2" (5cm)   14" (36cm)   2" (5cm)

Pet Collar and Leash *beginner*

Keep your pet safe with this must-have, glow-in-the-dark Pet Collar and Leash. Green Peppermint Glow Jelly Yarn makes your pet easy to spot at night. The simple knit-into-the-back loop stitch gives the collar and leash added strength, yet it is both comfortable and cute. Knit different colors for all your pets, including the "stuffed" ones!

Yarn

1 ball Fine Jelly Yarn
Color: Green Peppermint Glow
85yds (78m) / 200g (100% vinyl)

Needles

US 6 (4mm) needles.

Gauge

Gauge not important for this project.

Stitch Guide

Knit through the Back Loop page 104

Slip a Stitch Purlwise page 105

Whipstitch page 118

Materials

¾" (2cm) Buckle

2 – Swivel clips

Tapestry needle

Finished Measurements

About ½" (1cm) wide

Pet Collar and Leash Patterns

Pet Collar Pattern

collaR

Cast on 4 stitches.

Leave 7" (18cm) for sewing to buckle.

- Tie a double knot after the last cast on stitch with the tail and yarn ball strands.

- To make an even edge, slip the 1st stitch of every row purlwise.

Row 1: Slip the 1st stitch purlwise, then knit through the back loop of each stitch across the row.

Repeat Row 1 for desired length—circumference around neck of pet, plus 4" (10cm) for overlap.

Bind off loosely.

Block piece flat.

Finishing

Sewing to Buckle
Thread tapestry needle with remaining yarn tail from cast on end and sew to buckle, using a whipstitch. Sew 3 stitches on each side of the tine.

Band

- This little band is used to keep the overlapping end in place after the collar is buckled.

Cast on 3 stitches.

Leave 4" (10cm) for sewing edges together.

- Tie a double knot after the last cast on stitch with the tail and yarn ball strands.

- To make an even edge, slip the 1st stitch of every row purlwise.

Row 1: Slip the 1st stitch purlwise, then knit through the back loop of each stitch across the row.

Repeat Row 1 for 3" (8cm).

Bind off loosely.

Finishing

Sewing Together
Turn band wrong side up. Thread tapestry needle with remaining yarn tail from cast on end, sew cast on, and bind off edges together, using a whipstitch. Turn right side out. Slide band onto collar, then 1st swivel clip.

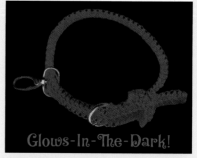

Glows-In-The-Dark!

Leash Pattern

Leash

Cast on 4 stitches.

Leave 7" (18cm) for sewing handle loop.

- *Tie a double knot after the last cast on stitch with the tail and yarn ball strands.*

- *To make an even edge, slip the 1st stitch of every row purlwise.*

Row 1: Slip the 1st stitch purlwise, then knit through the back loop of each stitch across the row.

Repeat Row 1 for 38" (97cm) or desired length.

Bind off loosely. Leave 7" (18cm) for sewing to swivel hook.

Block piece flat.

Finishing

Sewing Leash Handle

Thread tapestry needle with remaining yarn tail from cast on end. Fold cast on end over 5" (12cm) to form a loop and sew to leash, using a whipstitch.

Sewing Leash to Swivel Clip

Thread tapestry needle with remaining yarn tail from bind off end and sew to 2nd swivel hook bar, using a whipstitch.

- *Sew around metal bar evenly, covering it completely.*

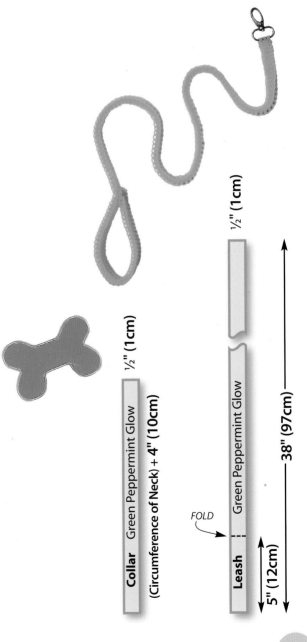

½" (1cm)

Collar   Green Peppermint Glow

(Circumference of Neck) + 4" (10cm)

½" (1cm)

Leash   Green Peppermint Glow

FOLD

38" (97cm)

5" (12cm)

Jump Rope

Jumping rope will never be as much fun as with this glow-in-the-dark Jump Rope featuring Green Peppermint and Pink Peppermint Glow Jelly Yarns. Knit simple one color or two color striped I-cord jump ropes with easy-to-make adjustable handles to fit any size hand. The glow-in-the-dark yarns are designed to provide hours of fun for everyone, both day and night.

Stitch Guide
I-Cord page 104

Needles
US 8 (5mm) double pointed needles.

Yarn
1 ball Bulky Jelly Yarn
Color: Green Peppermint Glow
65yds (60m) / 240g (100% vinyl)

1 ball Bulky Jelly Yarn
Color: Pink Peppermint Glow
65yds (60m) / 240g (100% vinyl)

Gauge
Gauge not important for this project.

Materials
Tapestry needle

Finished Measurements
About ½" wide x 100" (1cm x 254cm) long

Jump Rope Patterns

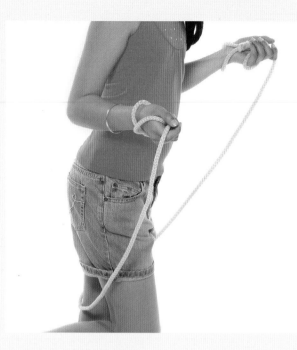

Two Color Striped Jump Rope Pattern

I-cord Jump Rope

With Pink Peppermint Glow, cast on 3 stitches. Leave 20" (50cm) for sewing handle loop.

- *Tie a double knot after the last cast on stitch with the tail and yarn ball strands.*

Row 1: Without turning needle, slide stitches to the right point. Join Green Peppermint Glow with a double knot and knit the 3 stitches across.

- *Pull yarn tightly after the 1st knit stitch.*

- *Be careful not to slide stitches off the needle.*

Row 2: Without turning needle, slide stitches to the right point. Do not cut Green Peppermint Glow. With Pink Peppermint Glow, knit the 3 stitches across.

- *To help make the stitches even and close up the I-cord, give the green and pink yarns a little tug as you knit.*

Row 3: Without turning needle, slide stitches to the right point. With Green Peppermint Glow, knit the 3 stitches across.

- *Pull yarns tightly after the 1st knit stitch.*

Row 4: Without turning needle, slide stitches to the right point. With Pink Peppermint Glow, knit the 3 stitches across.

- *Pull yarns tightly after the 1st knit stitch.*

Repeat Rows 3 and 4 for a total of 100" (254cm) or desired length.

- *Pull yarns tightly on the 1st knit stitch of every row.*

Bind off tightly. Make a double tight knot with the 2 strand colors. Trim Green Peppermint Glow.

Leave 20" (50cm) of Pink Peppermint Glow for sewing handle loop.

- *Do not block!*

- *Pull and stretch to even out stitches.*

Glows-In-The-Dark!

Finishing

Sewing Handle Loop

Fold 6" (15cm) from cast on end to form a loop. Thread tapestry needle with yarn. Wrap with the end and the rope together for 1" (4cm). Keep the yarn strands even and straight.

Slide needle though center of wrap, pull through, and tie a double knot. Trim ends. Repeat on bind off end.

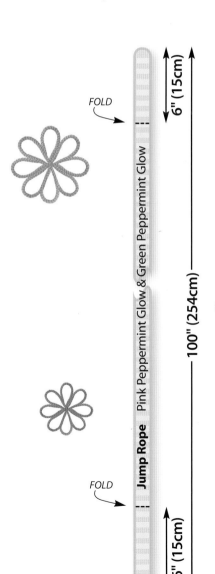

FOLD

6" (15cm)

Jump Rope   Pink Peppermint Glow & Green Peppermint Glow

100" (254cm)

FOLD

6" (15cm)

One Color Jump Rope Pattern

I-cord Jump Rope

With Green Peppermint Glow, cast on 3 stitches. Leave 20" (50cm) for sewing handle loop.

• *Tie a double knot after the last cast on stitch with the tail and yarn ball strands.*

Row 1: Without turning needle, slide stitches to the right point and knit the 3 stitches across.

• *Pull yarn tightly after the 1st knit stitch.*

• *Be careful not to slide stitches off the needle.*

Repeat Row 1 for 100" (254cm).

Bind off tightly. Leave 20" (50cm) for sewing handle loop.

• *Do not block!*

• *Pull and stretch to even out stitches.*

Finishing

Sewing Handle Loop

Fold 6" (15cm) from cast on end to form a loop. Thread tapestry needle with remaining yarn tail. Wrap the end and the rope together for 1½" (4cm). Keep the yarn strands even and straight. Slide needle though center of wrap, pull through, and tie a double knot. Trim ends. Repeat on bind off end.

Fun Belt

easy

Knit a super cool belt by mixing Blue Taffy and Green Peppermint Glow Jelly Yarns in a simple design. Make the Fun Belt by sewing two I-cords together. Choose your favorite color combinations. It's fun to mix and match Jelly Yarns to create a jelly belt to go with any outfit. What are your favorite Jelly Yarn colors?

Stitch Guide
I-Cord page 104

Whipstitch page 118

Needles
US 8 (5mm) double pointed needles, or size needed to obtain gauge.

Yarn
1 ball Bulky Jelly Yarn
Color: Green Peppermint Glow
65yds (60m) / 240g (100% vinyl)

1 ball Bulky Jelly Yarn
Color: Blue Taffy
65yds (60m) / 240g (100% vinyl)

Gauge
Alert! Make sure all 3 I-cords fit side by side into your belt buckle.

Materials
Belt buckle with a 1½" (4cm) opening

Tapestry needle

Finished Measurements
1½" (4cm) wide

Size
Size to fit.

Fun Belt Pattern

With Blue Taffy, cast on 3 stitches.

- *Tie a double knot after the last cast on stitch with the tail and yarn ball strands.*

Row 1: Without turning needle, slide stitches to the right point and knit the 3 stitches across.

- *Be careful not to slide stitches off the needle.*

Repeat Row 1 for the length of your measurement.

- *Remember to pull yarn tightly after the 1st knit stitch.*

Bind off tightly. Leave 8" (20cm) for sewing to the buckle.

- *Do not block!*

Belt-Short I-cord

Find Your Measurement for the Short I-cord Piece:
Measure your hips. Add 6" (15cm) for overlap.

Hip Measurement Guide
Size 7:   27" (69cm) + 6" (15cm) = 33" (84cm)
Size 8:   28" (71cm) + 6" (15cm) = 34" (86cm)
Size 10: 30" (76cm) + 6" (15cm) = 36" (91cm)
Size 12: 32" (81cm) + 6" (15cm) = 38" (97cm)
Size 14: 34" (86cm) + 6" (15cm) = 40" (101cm)
Size 16: 36" (91cm) + 6" (15cm) = 42" (107cm)

With Green Peppermint Glow, cast on 3 stitches.

- *Tie a double knot after the last cast on stitch with the tail and yarn ball strands.*

Row 1: Without turning needle, slide stitches to the right point and knit the 3 stitches across.

- *Be careful not to slide stitches off the needle.*

Repeat Row 1 for the length of your measurement.

- *Remember to pull yarn tightly after the 1st knit stitch.*

Bind off tightly.

- *Do not block!*

Belt-Long I-cord

Find Your Measurement for the Long I-cord Piece:
Measure your hips. Multiply by 2 and add 6" (15cm) for overlap.

Hip Measurement Guide
Size 7:   27" (69cm) x 2 = 54" (137cm) + 6" (15cm) = 60" (152cm)
Size 8:   28" (71cm) x 2 = 56" (142cm) + 6" (15cm) = 62" (157cm)
Size 10: 30" (76cm) x 2 = 60" (152cm) + 6" (15cm) = 66" (168cm)
Size 12: 32" (81cm) x 2 = 64" (163cm) + 6" (15cm) = 70" (178cm)
Size 14: 34" (86cm) x 2 = 68" (173cm) + 6" (15cm) = 74" (188cm)
Size 16: 36" (91cm) x 2 = 72" (183cm) + 6" (15cm) = 78" (198cm)

Finishing

Sewing I-cords Together

Fold Blue Taffy long I-cord in half on a flat surface and keep straight.

Place Green Peppermint Glow short I-cord in the center of the folded Blue Taffy I-cord and keep straight.

Thread tapestry needle with a strand of Blue Taffy yarn approximately 3 times longer than your belt. Sew into the top loops of the 3 I-cord pieces on the wrong side, joining the I-cords together in a zigzag motion.

* *Do not pull the yarn too tightly, or the I-cords will curl.*

Sewing Belt to Buckle

Thread tapestry needle with remaining yarn tail from Blue Taffy end and sew to buckle, using a whipstitch.

* *Place an even amount of stitches on both sides of the tine.*

Glows-In-The-Dark!

Belt	Long I-Cord	Blue Taffy	1½" (4cm)
60 (62, 66, 70, 74, 78)"	152 (157, 168, 178, 188, 198)cm		

Belt	Short I-Cord	Green Peppermint Glow	1½" (4cm)
33 (34, 36, 38, 40, 42)"	84 (86, 91, 97, 101, 107)cm		

Feather Party Purse *easy*

A fluffy, lightweight boa and juicy Raspberry Sorbet Jelly Yarn make the Feather Party Purse a must-have accessory for any occasion. This easy-to-knit bag uses a basic garter stitch. Assembly is easy; fold the bag in half, sew the side seams together, and attach the cool boa shoulder strap. You'll be amazed at how much fun it is to knit and wear!

Stitch Guide

Knit Stitch (K) page 103

Whipstitch page 118

Needles

US 8 (5mm) needles.

Gauge

Gauge not important for this project.

Yarn

1 ball Bulky Jelly Yarn
Color: Raspberry Sorbet
65yds (60m) / 240g (100% vinyl)

Finished Measurements

About 6" wide x 6" high (15cm x 15cm)

Materials

Pink feather boa

Sewing needle

Pink sewing thread (matching feather boa)

Tapestry needle

Feather Party Purse Pattern

Begin bind off on same side as cast on tail.

Bind off loosely. Leave 18" (46cm) for sewing side seams.

• *Stretch yarn to even out the stitches.*

Block piece flat.

Front and Back

Cast on 23 stitches. Leave 18" (46cm) for sewing side seams.

• *Tie a double knot after the last cast on stitch with the tail and yarn ball strands.*

Row 1: Knit across the row.

Repeat Row 1 for 12" (30cm).

Finishing

Sewing Side Seams

Fold the bag in half with the wrong side out. Thread tapestry needle with remaining yarn from the cast on tail. Align side seams and sew, using a whipstitch. Sew other side seam, using remaining yarn tail from bind off. Turn purse right side out.

Shoulder Strap

Insert a 2" (5cm) end of the boa inside the top right seam of the purse. With matching thread and sewing needle, sew boa around the top edge of the purse.

- *Be sure to push the needle through the core of the boa to attach securely.*

Measure 40" (101cm) or desired length for shoulder strap. For a shorter purse handle, see Alternate Short Purse Handle. Wrap with tape and cut. Sew the other end of the boa inside the top left seam of the purse.

Alternate Short Purse Handle

Measure 15" (38cm) or desired length for handle strap. Wrap with tape and cut. Sew the other end of the boa inside the top left seam of the purse.

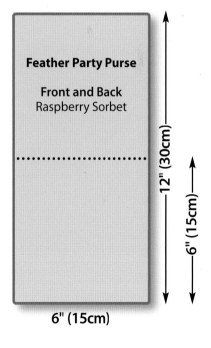

Feather Party Purse

Front and Back
Raspberry Sorbet

12" (30cm)

6" (15cm)

6" (15cm)

Jewelry Box

Treasure your most precious jewels in your own Honey Gold Jewelry Box. Create five easy to knit squares using a simple knit-through-the-back-loop stitch. You'll love having a special place to store your favorite charms, bracelets, and rings. Decorate with four large crystal rhinestones and fill this golden jewelry box with your favorite gems!

Needles
US 8 (5mm) needles.

Gauge
Gauge not important for this project.

Yarn

1 ball Fine Jelly Yarn
Color: Honey Gold
85yds (78m) / 200g (100% vinyl)

Stitch Guide
Knit through the Back Loop page 104

Slip a Stitch Purlwise page 105

Whipstitch page 118

Finished Folded Measurements
About 3½" wide x 3½" high x 1½" deep (9cm x 9cm x 4cm)

Materials
4 – Rhinestone crystals

Tapestry needle

Jewelry Box Pattern

Bind off loosely. Leave 12" (30cm) for sewing seams.

• *All 5 pieces should be the same square size.*

Block the 5 pieces flat.

Finishing

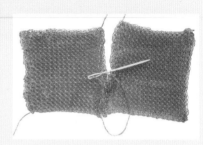

Sewing Side Seams

With wrong sides out, place side of 1st piece along side of 2nd piece. Thread tapestry needle with 12" (30cm) of yarn and sew sides together, using a whipstitch.

Position side of 3rd piece along side of 2nd piece and sew sides together.

Position side of 4th piece along side of 3rd piece and sew sides together. Sew 1st piece and 4th piece together to form a bottomless box.

Sides or Bottom *(make 5 pieces)*

Cast on 18 stitches. Leave 12" (30cm) for sewing seams.

• *Tie a double knot after the last cast on stitch with the tail and yarn ball strands.*

• *To make an even edge, slip the 1st stitch of every row purlwise.*

Row 1: Slip the 1st stitch purlwise, then knit through the back loop of each stitch across the row.

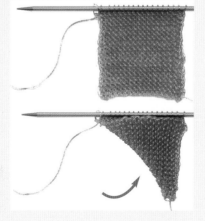

Repeat Row 1 until square. Check square shape by folding knitting on an angle. When the bottom corner reaches the top corner, the piece is square.

Sewing Bottom of Box

Place 5th piece in position for the bottom of the box. Thread tapestry needle with 20" (51cm) of yarn and sew 4 edges of box and 5th piece together closing the bottom of the box.

- *Tie a double knot with remaining strands and trim ends.*

Fold Down Sides

Keep wrong side out and turn the box upside down, so the top is open. Fold sides out and down, with right side facing out.

Thread tapestry needle with 20" (51cm) of yarn and sew top edges to the bottom edges of the box.

Attach Crystal Rhinestones

Cut a 4" (10cm) piece of yarn. Thread through ring on crystal and tie to the box corner with a tight double knot. Trim edges. Repeat for 3 remaining corners.

Jewelry Box

Sides or Bottom
(make 5 pieces)
Honey Gold

3 ½" (9cm)

3½" (9cm)

Mini Purse

easy

From money to music pods, the Mini Purse is great for every little purpose! Knit with Lemon-Lime Ice and Blue Taffy Jelly Yarns for a perfect two-tone match. No decreasing either; just fold and sew your knitted rectangle to form the easy pointed flap. Mix and match your favorite colors for a fun knitting experience!

Stitch Guide

Knit through the Back Loop page 104

Slip a Stitch Purlwise page 105

Whipstitch page 118

Needles

US 8 (5mm) needles.

Yarn

1 ball Fine Jelly Yarn
Color: Lemon-Lime Ice
85yds (78m) / 200g (100% vinyl)

1 ball Fine Jelly Yarn
Color: Blue Taffy
85yds (78m) / 200g (100% vinyl)

Gauge

Gauge not important
for this project.

Finished Measurements

About 4½" wide x 3" high
(11cm x 8cm)

Materials

½" (1cm) Metal snap

Decorative button (optional)

Tapestry needle

Invisible thread

Sewing needle

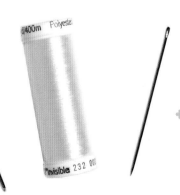

Mini Purse Pattern

Shoulder Strap

With Blue Taffy, cast on 4 stitches.

Leave 8" (20cm) for sewing the strap to the purse.

• *Tie a double knot after the last cast on stitch with the tail and yarn ball strands.*

• *To make an even edge, slip the 1st stitch of every row purlwise.*

Row 1: Slip the 1st stitch purlwise, then knit through the back loop of each stitch across the row.

Repeat Row 1 for 11" (28cm) or desired length.

Change to Lemon-Lime Ice.

Repeat Row 1 for 11" (28cm).

Change to Blue Taffy.

Repeat Row 1 for 11" (28cm).

Bind off loosely. Leave 8" (20cm) for sewing the strap to the purse.

Block piece flat.

Front and Back

Make a slip knot 25" (63cm) from the tail end.

With Blue Taffy, cast on 16 stitches.

• *Tie a double knot after the last cast on stitch with the tail and yarn ball strands.*

• *To make an even edge, slip the 1st stitch of every row purlwise.*

Row 1: Slip the 1st stitch purlwise, then knit through the back loop of each stitch across the row.

Repeat Row 1 for 4½" (11cm).

Change to Lemon-Lime Ice.

Repeat Row 1 for 4½" (11cm).

Bind off loosely. Leave 8" (20cm) for sewing the flap point.

Block piece flat.

Finishing

Sewing Flap Point

Place knitted piece on a flat surface. With wrong side out, fold corners of Lemon-Lime Ice edge to a point. Thread tapestry needle with remaining yarn tail from bind off and sew edges together, using a whipstitch.

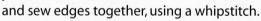

Sewing Inside Flap Edge

Next, insert needle at left flap corner and sew across to the right corner, using a whipstitch. Work in the top stitches to avoid sewing through the knitting to the other side.

Sewing Side Seams

Fold 2½" (6cm) of the Blue Taffy side up. Thread tapestry needle with remaining yarn tail from cast on. Make sides straight and even. Sew left side seam, using a whipstitch.

Make sure the needle goes through all 4 loops. Weave the yarn along the bottom edge from the left side to the right side. Sew up the right side seam, using a whipstitch. Turn purse right side out.

Sewing Shoulder Strap

With purse flap open, thread tapestry needle with remaining yarn tail from cast on and place end of strap 1" (2cm) inside the top left corner of the bag. Use a whipstitch and sew securely. Straighten strap and repeat for the other end, sewing to the top right corner of the bag.

Sewing on Snap

Thread sewing needle with 18" (46cm) of invisible thread. With the purse open, position the top snap, point side up, on the center of the Lemon-Lime Ice inside flap. Sew opening of snap to loop of stitch. Position the bottom snap, point side down, in the center of the Blue Taffy right side. Make sure the snaps line up. Sew bottom snap in position.

• *Check alignment after sewing each opening in snap.*

Sewing on Decorative Button (optional)

Position button on right side of flap near point. Sew button to loop of stitch.

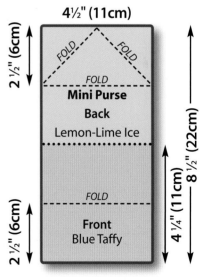

4½" (11cm)		

Mini Purse Back
Lemon-Lime Ice

Front
Blue Taffy

2½" (6cm) · 4¼" (11cm) · 8½" (22cm)

Blue Taffy	**Strap** Lemon-Lime Ice	Blue Taffy
11" (28cm)	11" (28cm)	11" (28cm)

33" (84cm)

½" (1cm)

Beach Bag

advanced beginner

You'll be cool at the shore carrying this striped Jelly Yarn Beach Bag! It knits up easily in the round with Lemon-Lime Ice and Hot Pink Candy Jelly Yarn on large circular needles. This durable, waterproof bag is the ideal companion for those warm days relaxing on the beach or at the pool. The bag expands, which makes it the perfect carryall for all your important stuff!

Needles

US 8 (5mm), US 15 (10mm) straight needles, and US 17 (12.75mm) 16" circular needles, or size needed to obtain gauge.

Yarn

1 ball Bulky Jelly Yarn
Color: Lemon-Lime Ice
65yds (60m) / 240g (100% vinyl)

1 ball Bulky Jelly Yarn
Color: Hot Pink Candy
65yds (60m) / 240g (100% vinyl)

Gauge

9 stitches and 12 rows = 4" (10cm) using size US 17 circular needles.

Materials

Tapestry needle

Stitch marker

Cord stop

Stitch Guide

Knit Stitch (K) page 103

Knit through the Back Loop page 104

Slip a Stitch Purlwise page 105

Knitting in the Round page 106

Whipstitch page 118

Running Stitch page 118

Finished Measurements

About 11" wide x 13" high (28cm x 33cm)

Beach Bag Pattern

- *Be careful not to twist your stitches.*
- *You are now working in rounds. Move marker with every round.*

Rounds 6–12: Knit through the back loop of each stitch around.

- *As you drop the used color yarn and change to a new color yarn, make a tight double knot before cutting the previous color.*

Rounds 13–21: Drop Lemon-Lime Ice and change to Hot Pink Candy. Knit through the back loop of each stitch around.

Rounds 22–30: Drop Hot Pink Candy and change to Lemon-Lime Ice. Knit through the back loop of each stitch around.

Rounds 31–39: Drop Lemon-Lime Ice and change to Hot Pink Candy. Knit through the back loop of each stitch around.

Bind off loosely. Leave 14" (36cm) for sewing bottom edge.

Block piece flat.

Front and Back

Make a slip knot 60" (152cm) from the tail end.

With US 15 straight needles, cast on 51 stitches with Lemon-Lime Ice.

- *Tie a double knot after the last cast on stitch with the tail and yarn ball strands.*

Rows 1–4: Knit across each row.

Row 5: Change to US 17 circular needles and knit through the back loop of each stitch around.

- *Straighten the stitches on the needle.*

Join by knitting 2 stitches together and pull tight!
Place a stitch marker (50 stitches).

Shoulder Strap

With US 8 straight needles, cast on 4 stitches with Lemon-Lime Ice. Leave 6" (15cm) for sewing to bag.

- *Tie a double knot after the last cast on stitch with the tail and yarn ball strands.*
- *To make an even edge, slip the 1st stitch purlwise.*

Row 1: Slip the 1st stitch purlwise, then knit through the back loop of each stitch across the row.

Repeat Row 1 for 14" (36cm).

Change to Hot Pink Candy yarn.

- *Tie a double knot with Lemon-Lime Ice and Hot Pink Candy.*

Repeat Row 1 for a total of 28" (71cm).

Bind off loosely. Leave 18" (46cm) for sewing strap to bag.

Block piece flat.

Finishing

Sewing Bottom Edges

Place knitted piece on a flat surface. With wrong side out, thread tapestry needle with remaining yarn strand from bind  off and sew bottom edges together securely, using a whipstitch. Double knot tail strand tightly.

Sewing Top Side Seam

Place knitted piece on a flat surface. With wrong side out, thread tapestry needle with remaining yarn strand from cast  on. Sew side seam from 1st 4 rows together securely, using a whipstitch. Double knot tail strand tightly.

Sewing Shoulder Strap

With right side out, place knitted piece on a flat surface. Thread tapestry needle with remaining Lemon-Lime Ice yarn strand from cast on. Using a whipstitch, sew the edge of strap to the top edge of the bag. Straighten strap and sew the bottom edge of the strap to the bottom edge of the bag.

Attaching Drawstring

Cut a 30" (76cm) strand of Hot Pink Candy. Thread tapestry needle with remaining yarn. Weave yarn through Row 5 of bag, using a running stitch, leaving both ends hanging together in front. Be sure to sew loosely enough for bag to open completely. Thread cord stop through  ends, and make a double knot at the end of each strand.

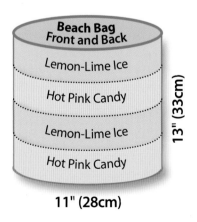

Beach Bag Front and Back

Lemon-Lime Ice

Hot Pink Candy

Lemon-Lime Ice

Hot Pink Candy

13" (33cm)

11" (28cm)

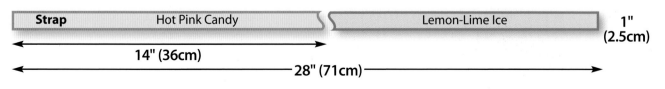

| **Strap** | Hot Pink Candy | Lemon-Lime Ice | 1" (2.5cm) |

14" (36cm)

28" (71cm)

Knapsack

advanced beginner

We combined juicy Raspberry Sorbet Jelly Yarn with a super soft aqua fiber yarn to create this smart-looking Knapsack for everyday casual wear. Two basic stitches, garter and stockinette, make this sturdy carryall an easy project to knit. The wide flap and flexible strap make it cool to use and enjoy!

Yarn

1 ball Fine Jelly Yarn
Color: Raspberry Sorbet
85yds (78m) / 200g (100% vinyl)

1 skein Lion Brand Homespun
Color: Waterfall 790-329
185yds (170m) / 170g (98% acrylic, 2% polyester)

Needles

US 10 (6mm), US 10½ (6.5mm), and US 11 (8mm) needles, or size needed to obtain gauge.

Gauge

12 stitches and 16 rows = 4" (10cm) with 1 strand of Jelly Yarn and 1 strand of Homespun held together using US 10½ needles.

Materials

Tapestry needle

Stitch Guide

Knit Stitch (K) page 103

Purl Stitch (P) page 105

Slip a Stitch Purlwise page 105

Whipstitch page 118

Finished Measurements

8" wide x 9" high (20cm x 23cm)

Knapsack Pattern

Front and Back

- *To prevent tangling, keep yarns separated.*
- *Tie a knot at the end of the Homespun to prevent fraying.*
- *Pull Jelly Yarn from outside of ball.*

With one strand each of Jelly Yarn and Homespun held together and US 10 needles, cast on 24 stitches.

- *Straighten stitches on needle.*

Rows 1–4: Knit across every row.

Change to US 10½ needles.

Row 5: (wrong side): Purl across.

Row 6: (right side): Knit across.

Repeat Rows 5 and 6 (stockinette stitch) for 18" (46cm), ending on a knit row.

For the flap, change to US 11 needles.

Knit across every row for 6" (15cm).

Bind off loosely.

Strap

- *Pull Jelly Yarn from outside and inside of ball.*

With two strands of Jelly Yarn held together and US 10 needles, cast on 4 stitches.

Leave 6" (15cm) for sewing strap to bag.

- *Tie a double knot after the last cast on stitch with the tail and yarn ball strands.*
- *To make an even edge, slip the 1st stitch of every row purlwise.*

Row 1: Slip the 1st stitch purlwise, then knit across the row.

Repeat Row 1 for 40" (101cm).

Bind off loosely. Leave 6" (15cm) for sewing strap to bag.

Finishing

Sewing Side Seams

With right side out, beginning at cast on edge, fold rows 1–4 over to outside. Thread tapestry needle with Homespun and sew the side edges of the folded portion in place to sides of bag, using a whipstitch.

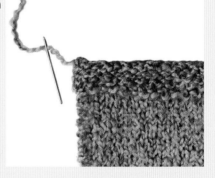

Fold the bag with the wrong side out so that the folded edge is lined up with the bottom of the flap. Thread tapestry needle with Homespun yarn. Align side seams and sew, using a whipstitch. Repeat for other side seam. Turn purse right side out.

Sewing Shoulder Strap

With purse flap open, thread tapestry needle with remaining yarn tail from cast on edge of strap. Place end of strap 1" (2.5cm) inside the top left corner of the bag. Use a whipstitch to sew securely to inside of the bag. Straighten strap and repeat for the other end, sewing to the top right corner of the bag.

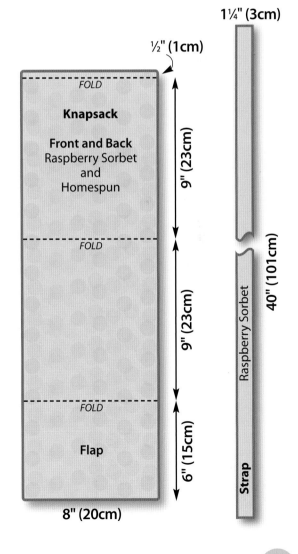

1¼" (3cm)

½" (1cm)

FOLD

Knapsack

Front and Back
Raspberry Sorbet
and
Homespun

9" (23cm)

FOLD

9" (23cm)

40" (101cm)

Raspberry Sorbet

FOLD

Flap

6" (15cm)

Strap

8" (20cm)

3

Crochet Jelly Yarn Projects

Glow Belt

beginner

Have fun crocheting this cute Glow Belt featuring Pink Peppermint Glow Jelly Yarn. This simple to crochet belt glows-in-the-dark, and is made with a basic single crochet stitch. Attach a large plastic buckle for a fun look. Stretch it over your coolest top, or weave it through the loops of your favorite jeans.

Stitch Guide

Chain (ch) page 110

Slip Stitch (sl st) page 111

Single Crochet (sc) page 112

Whipstitch page 118

Hook

US F/5 (3.75mm) and US H/8 (5mm) crochet hooks.

Yarn

1 ball Fine Jelly Yarn
Color: Pink Peppermint Glow
85yds (78m) / 200g (100% vinyl)

Gauge

Alert! Make sure your belt fits inside your buckle.

With smaller hook
4 stitches = 1" (2.5cm)

With smaller hook
21 rows = 4" (10cm)

Materials

Belt buckle with a 1¼" (3cm) opening

Tapestry needle

Finished Measurements

1" (2.5cm) wide x your hip measurement + 6" (15cm)

Size

Size to fit.

Glow Belt Pattern

With F hook, chain 5.

Row 1: Single crochet in the 2nd chain from hook and in each chain across the row. Turn.

Row 2: Chain 1, single crochet in the 1st stitch and in each stitch across the row. Turn.

Repeat Row 2 for the length of your measurement.

• *Do not fasten off.*

Chain 1, do not turn.

Change to size H hook.

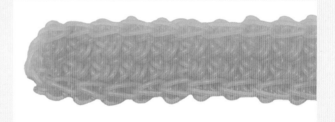

Belt

Find your measurement:
Measure your hips. Add 6" (15cm) for overlap.

Hip measurement guide:

Size 7: 27" (69cm) + 6" (15cm) = 33" (84cm)

Size 8: 28" (71cm) + 6" (15cm) = 34" (86cm)

Size 10: 30" (76cm) + 6" (15cm) = 36" (91cm)

Size 12: 32" (81cm) + 6" (15cm) = 38" (97cm)

Size 14: 34" (86cm) + 6" (15cm) = 40" (101cm)

Size 16: 36" (91cm) + 6" (15cm) = 42" (107cm)

Loosely slip stitch along top edge, around end working 2 slip stitches into each corner, and along bottom edge.

• *Work loosely so belt does not bunch up.*

Fasten off. Leave 8" (20cm) for sewing to the buckle.

Tie a double knot.

Block piece flat.

Finishing

Sewing Belt to Buckle

Thread a tapestry needle with remaining yarn tail and sew to buckle, using a whipstitch.

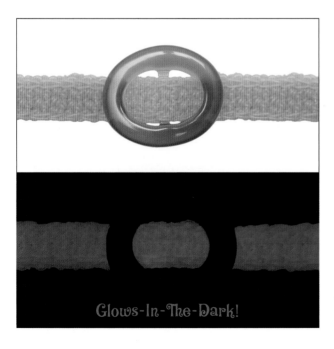

Glows-In-The-Dark!

1¼" (3cm)

Peppermint Glow

33 (34,36,38,40,42)" 84 (86,91,97,101,107)cm

Belt

Flying Jelly Ring

beginner & easy

You'll enjoy tossing around your very own Flying Jelly Ring featuring Blue Smoothie Jelly Yarn trimmed in Pink Parfait. First, we cut out bright felt rings, then crocheted around them to create this unique flying disc. Use your jelly stash yarn and crochet fun-tastic combinations. Try the musical variation by adding bells to create a one-of-a-kind tambourine!

Hook

US L/11 (8mm) crochet hook.

Gauge

Gauge not important for this project.

Yarn

6yds (5m) Bulky Jelly Yarn (Flying Jelly Ring) Color: Blue Smoothie 65yds (60m) / 240g (100% vinyl

6yds (5m) Bulky Jelly Yarn (Flying Jelly Ring) Color: Pink Parfait 65yds (60m) / 240g (100% vinyl)

12yds (11m) Bulky Jelly Yarn (Tambourine) Color: Silver Icing 65yds (60m) / 240g (100% vinyl)

Materials

9½" (24cm) diameter round plastic canvas

1 – 8" x 10" (20cm x 25cm) Red self-stick felt or foam sheet

1 – 8" x 10" (20cm x 25cm) Yellow self-stick felt or foam sheet

1 – 8" x 10" (20cm x 25cm) Blue self-stick felt or foam sheet (Tambourine)

5" (12cm) diameter metal craft ring (Tambourine)

10 – Large metal jingle bells (Tambourine)

Stitch Guide

Chain (ch) page 110

Slip Stitch (sl st) page 111

Single Crochet (sc) page 112

Finished Measurements

6½" (17cm) diameter

Leftovers!

This project is great for using leftover yarn because you don't need much.

Flying Jelly Ring Pattern

Flying Jelly Ring Pattern

- *Before crocheting, cut out the support ring to crochet the yarn around.*

Cutting Out the Support Ring

Cut one ring from circular plastic canvas with a 4" (10cm) inner diameter and 5⅝" (14cm) outer diameter.

- *The easy no-measure way is to use the grid lines of the plastic canvas: from the center of the circle, count out 14 rounds and cut along the 14th round. This is the inner edge of your ring; trim off the little spokes sticking out from the cut edge. For the outer edge of the ring, cut along the 6th round from the inner edge, and trim.*

Using the plastic ring as a guide, cut 1 red and 1 yellow ring from the self-stick foam or felt sheets. Affix the red and yellow felt rings to each side of the plastic canvas ring.

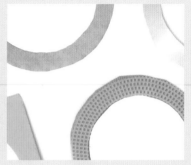

Crocheting the Ring

Round 1: With Blue Smoothie, make a slip knot and place loop on hook. Place hook into ring, yarn over and pull loop through ring (two loops on hook), yarn over, pull yarn over the top of the ring with a relaxed tension so that the ring doesn't bend, and through the two loops on the hook: one single crochet made around the ring.

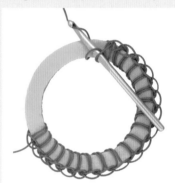

- *Make each single crochet tall enough to easily cover the ring by pulling the loops up high on the hook.*

Single crochet 29 more times around the ring. Crochet loosely so that the ring stays flat. Join round with slip stitch into 1st single crochet. (30 sc)

Fasten off and attach Pink Parfait with a slip stitch in the 1st single crochet, do not turn.

- *If you are using the same color for Round 2, do not turn.*

Round 2: Slip stitch in each single crochet around, slip stitch in 1st slip stitch to join round.

Fasten off. Tie a double knot. Trim ends.

Tambourine Pattern *easy*

- *In Round 2, stitches are worked into the front loop only of Round 1. The front loop is the top loop of the single crochet stitch that is closest to you.*

Cut out 2 blue felt or foam rings as described above. Affix the blue rings to each side of the 5" (12cm) metal craft ring.

- *Because of the metal ring and bells, this toy is designed for music, not for tossing.*

String 10 jingle bells onto Silver Icing Jelly Yarn and slide them down to approximately 6 yards (5m) from the slip knot. You will not need them until Round 2.

Round 1: Work the same as Round 1 for the Flying Jelly Ring. Turn.

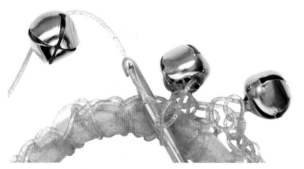

Round 2: *Chain 1, slide 1 bell close to hook, chain 1 (bell is included in the stitch), chain 1, slip stitch in the front loop of the next single crochet, chain 1, slip stitch in front loop of next single crochet, chain 1, slip stitch in the next single crochet*, repeat from * to * around, ending round with a slip stitch in the 1st slip stitch to join.

Fasten off. Tie a double knot. Trim ends.

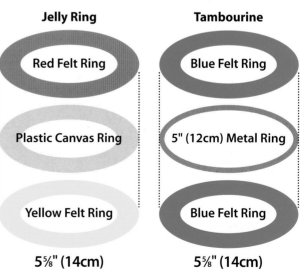

Jelly Ring	Tambourine
Red Felt Ring	Blue Felt Ring
Plastic Canvas Ring	5" (12cm) Metal Ring
Yellow Felt Ring	Blue Felt Ring
5⅝" (14cm)	5⅝" (14cm)

Hair Accessories

beginner & easy

Learn to crochet fun Hair Accessories with colorful Jelly Yarn. Use Raspberry Sorbet, Hot Pink Candy, and Lemon-Lime Ice colors to make the Flower Clasp and the Beaded Clip Barrettes. Make a sparkling Tiara with Silver Icing Jelly Yarn for all those special parties. You'll love the different hairstyles you can wear with these fun, easy-to-crochet Jelly Yarn gems!

Hook

US I/9 (5.5mm) crochet hook.

Gauge

Gauge not important for this project.

Yarn

Flower Clasp Barrette
**1 ball Fine Jelly Yarn
Color: Raspberry Sorbet
85yds (78m) / 200g (100% vinyl)**

Beaded Clip Barrette / Flower Clasp Barrette
**1 ball Fine Jelly Yarn
Color: Lemon-Lime Ice
85yds (78m) / 200g (100% vinyl)**

Beaded Clip Barrette / Flower Clasp Barrette
**1 ball Fine Jelly Yarn
Color: Hot Pink Candy
85yds (78m) / 200g (100% vinyl)**

Beaded Tiara
**1 ball Fine Jelly Yarn
Color: Silver Icing
85yds (78m) / 200g (100% vinyl)**

Materials

Flower Clasp Barrette
2½" (6cm) Automatic clasp barrette

Beaded Clip Barrette
**2 – 3" (8cm) Oval clip barrettes
21 – (7mm) Round glass beads, mixed colors**

Beaded Tiara
**Comb headband with 37 teeth
36 – (7mm) Pink round glass beads
Tapestry needle**

Stitch Guide

Chain (ch) page 110

Slip Stitch (sl st) page 111

Single Crochet (sc) page 112

Double Crochet (dc) page 113

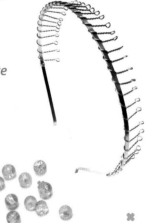

Leftovers!

This project is great for using leftover yarn because you don't need much.

Hair Accessories Pattern

Flower Clasp Barrette Pattern

(make 3 pieces)

easy

Raspberry Sorbet Flower

With Raspberry Sorbet yarn, chain 4 (counts as 1st double crochet and chain 1). *Double crochet in the 4th chain from hook, chain 1, repeat from * 6 times in the same chain. Counting up from the bottom, join with a slip stitch to the 3rd chain of the 1st 4 chains.

Fasten off. Leave a 5" (12cm) yarn tail to tie to the barrette.

Thread tapestry needle with the remaining yarn tail. Insert needle in bottom loops of all eight double crochet stitches and pull tightly to gather the flower together. Make a tight double knot.

Lemon-Lime Ice Flower

Repeat pattern above with Lemon-Lime Ice yarn.

Hot Pink Candy Flower

Repeat pattern above with Hot Pink Candy yarn.

Finishing

Attaching Flowers to Barrettes

Thread tapestry needle with the remaining yarn from Raspberry Sorbet flower. Open automatic clasp barrette with the hinge to the right, flat side facing up. Hold flower centered on the top of the flat barrette bar. Wind the yarn under the bar and insert needle through the base of the flower. Pull tight. Repeat. Tie a tight double knot at the base of the flower. Slide flower to the right. Repeat with the Lemon-Lime Ice flower. Slide the flower to the left. Repeat with the Hot Pink Candy flower in the center.

Beaded Clip Barrette Pattern

Hot Pink Candy Barrette

Hold the back of the barrette with the clip side up and hinge to your right. Open the clip.

With Hot Pink Candy yarn, make a slip stitch around the barrette bar on the right corner of the clip. Secure a tight double knot on the outside of the bar.

Flip the barrette with the oval side up and the clip hinge to the right.

Slide the hook under the 2 oval bars and yarn over. Bring the hook back over the top of the oval bars and make a single crochet. Single crochet evenly 11 more times around the barrette without overlapping the stitches.

Fasten off. Leave 8" (20cm) for stringing the beads.

Lemon-Lime Ice Barrette

Repeat pattern above with Lemon-Lime Ice yarn.

Finishing

Attaching Beads

String 7 different color beads on the tail end of the Hot Pink Candy barrette. Tie a tight double knot 6" (15cm) from the end of the barrette, or desired length. Trim yarn end.

Repeat for the Lemon-Lime Ice barrette.

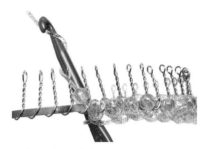

Slide bead to hook, bring hook under band between the 1st and 2nd tooth of the comb, and yarn over.

* *Keep the bead on the band and don't let it slide down the yarn.*

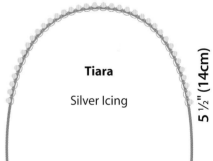

Bring the hook back under the band and make a single crochet.

Repeat around each tooth along the comb.

Fasten off. Make a tight double knot.

Beaded Tiara Pattern

Tiara

String 36 round pink beads on Silver Icing yarn.

Make a slip knot. Hold the hair comb with the band facing you. Beginning on the right, make a slip stitch around the band before the 1st tooth of the comb.

Tiara

Silver Icing

5 ½" (14cm)

Beaded Clip Barrette

Lemon-Lime Ice
Hot Pink Candy

6" (15cm)

1" (2.5cm)

Clasp Barrette Flowers

Lemon-Lime Ice
Raspberry Sorbet
Hot Pink Candy

Jelly Boot Sleeves

beginner & easy

Here's a rainy day project that you can use in the rain. Brighten up rubber rain boots with cool Jelly Boot Sleeves. Waterproof Jelly Yarn makes it easy. Create a rectangle in simple single and double crochet with Lemon-Lime Ice. Sew an easy side seam and attach large decorative flower buttons. Stretches to fit most kids' size boots. Try the alternate pattern with a ruffle!

Hook

US K/10.5 (6.5mm) crochet hook, or size needed to obtain gauge.

Gauge

Alert! Make sure your foundation chain fits snugly around your boots without stretching too much.
12 stitches and 9 rows = 4" (10cm)

Yarn

1 ball Fine Jelly Yarn
Color: Lemon-Lime Ice
85yds (78m) / 200g (100% vinyl)

Stitch Guide

Chain (ch) page 110

Single Crochet (sc) page 112

Double Crochet (dc) page 113

Whipstitch page 118

Finished Measurements

6" wide x 4" high (15cm x 10cm)

6" wide x 4½" (15cm x 11cm) (Ruffled Jelly Boot Sleeves)

Size

One size fits most kids' boots (S, M, L)

Materials

8 – Flower buttons

Pair of rubber rain boots (kids' size)

Tapestry needle

Safety pins

Leftovers!

This project is great for using leftover yarn because you don't need much.

Jelly Boot Sleeves Pattern

Front or Back *(make 2 pieces)*

Chain 39, or chain a length to fit around the circumference of the boot.

Row 1: Single crochet in the 2nd chain from hook and in each chain across the row. Chain 1. Turn. (38 sc)

Row 2: Single crochet in each stitch across the row. Chain 1. Turn.

Row 3: Single crochet in each stitch across the row. Chain 3. Turn.

Rows 4–5: Double crochet in each stitch across the row. Chain 3. Turn.

Row 6: Double crochet in each stitch across the row. Chain 1. Turn.

Rows 7–8: Repeat row 2.

Row 9: Single crochet in each stitch across the row. Fasten off. Tie a double knot.

Leave 8" (20cm) tail for sewing the side seam.

Block pieces flat.

Finishing

Sewing Seams Together

Wrap sleeve securely around right boot. Make sides straight and even, then pin together.

Remove sleeve from boot. With wrong side out, place rectangular piece on a flat surface. Fold sleeve in half across the width and pin side seams together with safety pins. Thread the yarn tail through the tapestry needle. Sew side seams together, using a whipstitch.

Repeat for left boot sleeve.

Attaching the Buttons

Right Side

Place sewn sleeve, right side out, on a flat surface with the seam on the left. Cut 4 strands of 8" (20cm) jelly yarn. Thread each end of the strand through each hole in the 1st button. Thread a

second strand through the second button. Center the two flower buttons ½" (1cm) apart on one side of the sleeve. With the crochet hook on the inside, pull the two strands of each button through to the inside. Make a tight double knot. Trim ends.

Repeat for the 2 remaining buttons on the other side of the sleeve.

Left Side

Place sewn sleeve, right side out, on flat surface with the seam on the right. Repeat the directions as written for the Right Side.

Ruffled Jelly Boot Sleeves Pattern *easy*

FRONT OR BACK *(make 2 pieces)*

Chain 39, or chain a length to fit around the circumference of the boot.

Row 1: Single crochet in the 2nd chain from hook and in each chain across the row. Chain 1. Turn. (38 sc)

Row 2: Single crochet in each stitch across the row. Chain 1. Turn.

Row 3: Single crochet in each stitch across the row. Chain 3. Turn.

Rows 4–5: Double crochet in each stitch across the row. Chain 3. Turn.

Row 6: Double crochet in each stitch across the row. Chain 1. Turn.

Rows 7–8: Repeat row 2.

Row 9: Single crochet in each stitch across the row. Do not fasten off. Turn.

Ruffle Edge

Row 10: Chain 3 (counts as the 1st double crochet), 2 double crochet in the 1st stitch, make 3 double crochet in each of the remaining stitches across the row. (114 dc)

Fasten off. Tie a double knot.

Leave 8" (20cm) tail for sewing the side seam.

Block pieces flat, except ruffled edge.

Finishing

• *Use finishing instructions from the previous pattern.*

Boot Sleeve

(make 2 pieces)
Lemon-Lime Ice

4" (10cm)

12" (30cm)

74

Sports Bottle Sling

easy

You'll love to crochet this easy Sports Bottle Sling using Blue Taffy Jelly Yarn. This fun tote is worked in the round and features an easy chain-5 stitch and single crochet. It's a handy way to keep your favorite drinks close-at-hand, and it's waterproof too. You'll enjoy hours of hands-free fun!

Hook

US I/9 (5.5mm) crochet hook.

Yarn

1 ball Fine Jelly Yarn
Color: Blue Taffy
85yds (78m) / 200g (100% vinyl)

Gauge

Gauge not important for this project.

Stitch Guide

Chain (ch) page 110

Slip Stitch (sl st) page 111

Single Crochet (sc) page 112

Single Crochet Around a Ring page 112

Whipstitch page 118

Finished Measurements

3" wide x 6" high (8cm x 15cm), not including strap

Materials

3 – 1" (2.5cm) Blue plastic rings
Stitch marker
Tapestry needle

Sports Bottle Sling Pattern

Sling

Round 1: Make a slip knot with a double knot and join with a slip stitch to the 1st ring, chain 1, make 11 single crochet stitches around the ring. Join with a slip stitch to the 1st stitch. Place a stitch marker.

Round 2: *Chain 5, single crochet in the next stitch, repeat from * around the ring. Move the stitch marker to the last stitch made. (10 chain-5)

Round 3: *Chain 5, single crochet in chain-5 space, repeat from * around to marker. Move the stitch marker to the last stitch made. Make sure you have 10 chain-5 spaces.

- *You will be working in a spiral. Do not turn or join.*

- *It's important to move the stitch marker with every round.*

Repeat round 3 for 6" (15cm) about 6 rounds, to marker and join with a slip stitch in 1st single crochet.

Make sure you have 10 chain-5 spaces every round.

Insert bottle to check bottle height. Add 1 round if too short or remove 1 round if too high.

Last Round: *2 single crochet in the chain-5 space, 1 single crochet in the next single crochet, repeat from * once around.

Fasten off. Leave 6" (15cm) for sewing to the strap ring.

- *Do not remove marker.*

Strap

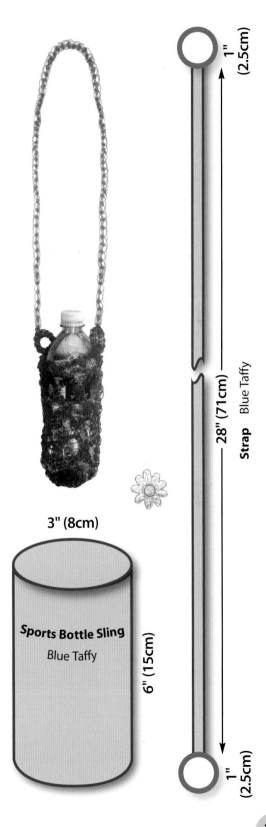

Row 1: Join yarn with a slip stitch to the 2nd ring. Chain 1, make 11 single crochet stitches around the ring. Join with a slip stitch to the 1st stitch. Chain 100 loosely.

Row 2: Attach 3rd ring with a slip stitch around the ring, chain 1, make 11 single crochet stitches around the ring.

• *Straighten the strap.*

Join with a slip stitch in the 100th chain. Slip stitch into the big (bottom) loop of every chain back along the strap. Join with a slip stitch to single crochet on 2nd ring.

Fasten off. Leave 6" (15cm) for sewing to the sling.

Finishing

Attaching the Strap to Sling

Thread tapestry needle with remaining yarn tail from 2nd ring and whipstitch ring and sling edge at marker, together. On opposite side, thread tapestry needle with remaining yarn tail from sling, straighten strap, and whipstitch to 3rd ring to sling edge together.

1" (2.5cm)

28" (71cm)   **Strap** Blue Taffy

1" (2.5cm)

3" (8cm)

Sports Bottle Sling
Blue Taffy

6" (15cm)

Jelly Bracelets

beginner & easy

Be cool with clear Ice Jelly Bracelets that stretch to fit over your wrist. Add different color rings to match any mood or outfit. We used an easy single crochet stitch to create these one-piece flexible bracelets. Use a simple slip stitch to decorate the colorful bangle bracelets with juicy Raspberry Sorbet Jelly Yarn. You'll enjoy crocheting these fun Jelly Yarn bracelets with and for your friends!

Stitch Guide

Chain (ch) page 110

Slip Stitch (sl st) page 111

Single Crochet (sc) page 112

Single Crochet Around a Ring page 112

Whipstitch page 118

Hook

US H/8 (5mm) crochet hook.

Yarn

1 ball Fine Jelly Yarn
Color: Ice
85yds (78m) / 200g (100% vinyl)

1 ball Fine Jelly Yarn
Color: Raspberry Sorbet
85yds (78m) / 200g (100% vinyl)

Gauge

Gauge not important for this project.

Materials

1" (2.5cm) Ring (blue)

2 – 1" (2.5cm) Ring (red)

½" (1cm) Green bangle bracelet

Finished Measurements

1" wide x 6" long (2.5 x 15cm)

Leftovers!

This project is great for using leftover yarn because you don't need much.

Jelly Bracelets Pattern

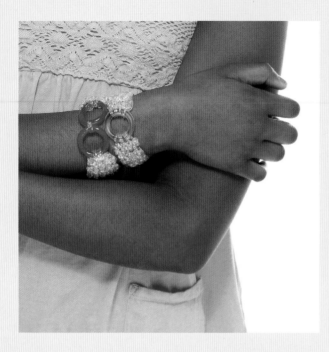

Row 1: Single crochet in each stitch across the row. Chain 1. Turn.

Repeat Row 1 for 6" (15cm) or desired length.

- *Bracelet will stretch to fit over hand.*

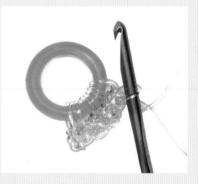

Last Row: Working over the opposite side of the same ring, single crochet in each stitch across the row.

Fasten off. Tie a double knot.

One Ring Bracelet Pattern

With Ice, make a slip knot with a double knot. Attach yarn with slip stitch to blue ring.

Foundation Row: Chain 1. Make 4 single crochet on the ring. Chain 1. Turn.

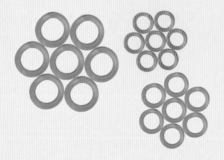

Two Ring Bracelet Pattern

With Ice, make a slip knot and tie a double knot. Attach yarn with slip stitch to 1st red ring.

Foundation Row: Chain 1. Make 4 single crochet on the 1st ring. Chain 1. Turn.

Row 1: Single crochet in each stitch across the row. Chain 1. Turn.

Repeat Row 1 for 6" (15cm) or desired length.

- *Bracelet will stretch to fit over hand.*

Last Row: Working over the 2nd red ring, single crochet in each stitch across the row.

Fasten off. Tie a double knot.

Finishing

Sewing Rings Together

Cut a 5" (12cm) length of yarn. Wind yarn around both rings 3 times and tie a double knot. Trim ends.

- *Add a drop of white glue to secure the knot.*

Jelly Bangle Bracelet Pattern *beginner*

With Raspberry Sorbet, make a slip knot and tie a double knot.

Make 1 slip stitch around the green bangle bracelet.

Repeat as many slip stitches as you desire around bangle bracelet and join with a slip stitch to the 1st stitch.

Fasten off. Tie a tight double knot.

- *Straighten or angle the stitches on the bracelet.*

1 Ring Bracelet
Ice

1" (2.5cm)

6" (15cm)

2 Ring Bracelet
Ice

1" (2.5cm)

6" (15cm)

Snow Globe Flower

easy

Here's something you can't do with fiber yarn. Make your own Snow Globe Flower featuring glow-in-the-dark, waterproof Jelly Yarn. Use Green and Pink Peppermint Glow Jelly Yarns to make these one-of-a-kind snow globes. These waterproof Jelly Yarn flowers are simple to crochet in the round, and they make great gifts for all your friends.

Stitch Guide

Chain (ch) page 110

Slip Stitch (sl st) page 111

Crochet a Center Ring page 111

Single Crochet (sc) page 112

Whipstitch page 118

Hook

US I/9 (5.5mm) crochet hook.

Gauge

Alert! Diameter of flower has to be no wider than 2½" (6cm) to fit inside snow globe dome.

Yarn

1 ball Fine Jelly Yarn
Color: Green Peppermint Glow
85yds (78m) / 200g (100% vinyl)

1 ball Fine Jelly Yarn
Color: Pink Peppermint Glow
85yds (78m) / 200g (100% vinyl)

Finished Measurements

2½" (6cm) diameter

Materials

3" (8cm) Make-it-yourself snow globe kit

Tapestry needle

Plastic model glue

Ear syringe (for filling snow globe)

Stitch marker

2½" diameter cup

Bowl for water

Leftovers!

This project is great for using leftover yarn because you don't need much.

Snow Globe Flower Pattern

Leaf Base

- *Work loosely.*

- *It's easier to see the 1st chain when you wrap the chain around your finger as you join the chain into a ring.*

Make a slip knot 8" (20cm) from yarn end.

With Green Peppermint Glow, chain 7, join with a slip stitch to the 1st chain to form a ring.

Round 1: Single crochet in center of ring, place marker on 1st stitch, make 9 more single crochet in center of ring. Join with a slip stitch to the marked stitch. (10 sc)

Round 2: Chain 1, make 10 single crochet stitches in the ring covering the previous round of stitches. Join with a slip stitch to the 1st stitch. (10 sc)

- *The ring should be very thick with the diameter of a quarter.*

Round 3: *Chain 3, single crochet in the next stitch, repeat from * around the ring. Join with a slip stitch to the 1st stitch. (10 sc)

Fasten off leaving an 8" (20cm) tail for sewing.

Tie a tight double knot with remaining yarn tails.

- *Make sure the leaf base fits inside the snow globe.*

Flower

- *Work loosely.*

- *It's easier to see the 1st chain when you wrap the chain around your finger as you join the chain into a ring.*

With Pink Peppermint Glow, crochet Flower using Rounds 1, 2, and 3 as Leaf Base.

- *Make sure the flower fits inside the snow globe.*

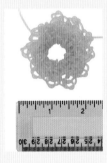

Finishing

Sewing Flower and Leaf Base Together

Place the bottom of the leaf base and flower facing, take the 2 remaining pink and green yarn strands of each, (total of 4 yarn strands) and tie together with a tight double knot.

Trim 2 pink and green yarn strands, leaving 2 yarn strands. Thread tapestry needle with remaining yarn strands and sew around the bottoms joining them together, using a whipstitch. Tie a tight double knot and trim end.

Gluing the Flower to the Inside of the Snow Globe

Place a nickel-sized amount of plastic model glue in the center of the snow globe base.

Place flower and leaf assemblage centered on top. Do not move.

Gluing the Snow Globe Dome

• *Make sure the flower fits inside of the snow globe dome BEFORE applying the glue!*

• *Place snow globe base on a paper towel or newspaper.*

Carefully squeeze an even bead of glue in the groove around the inside snow globe base.

• *This is important to ensure a watertight seal!*

Gently place your hand on top of the dome and hold for 30 seconds. Do not move.

Place a ball of jelly yarn or weight on top, and let it sit overnight to dry.

Filing the Snow Globe with Snow

Make sure the entire glued dome assembly is completely dry.

Place the globe upside down on a sturdy cup. Open the packet of snow flakes, included with the kit, and pour them inside the globe.

Filing the Snow Globe with Water

• *Cover the point of the plug with glue and have it ready to insert in the bottom of the globe base once it is filled with water.*

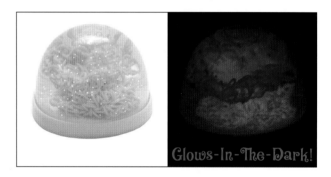

Here's the fun part! Fill a bowl with water.
Fill the ear syringe with water and insert the tip in the hole and expel the water. Repeat until the globe fills with water. Keep the tip of the syringe in the air bubble space when filling.

• *With the globe still upside down, tilt the globe so the tip of the syringe fills as much airspace as possible.*

When the air bubble is very small, insert the pre-glued plug in the hole firmly. Do not move. Let sit overnight to dry.

Glows-In-The-Dark!

Snow Globe Flower

2½" (6cm)	2½" (6cm)
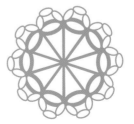	
Leaf Base	**Flower**
Green Peppermint Glow	Pink Peppermint Glow

Jelly Amigurumi Starfish *easy*

Amigurumi is a pop-culture crocheted toy from Japan. You'll have great fun making the Jelly Amigurumi Starfish with Blue Smoothie Jelly Yarn. Easily crocheted in the round, this eco-friendly pal has five tube-like legs attached to a round body. Add large animal eyes to complete the face.

Stitch Guide

Chain (ch) page 110

Slip Stitch (sl st) page 111

Crochet a Center Ring page 111

Single Crochet (sc) page 112

Decrease 2 Single Crochet (sc2tog) page 114

Whipstitch page 118

Hook

US J/10 (6mm) crochet hook.

Yarn

1 ball Fine Jelly Yarn
Color: Blue Smoothie
85yds (78m) / 200g (100% vinyl)

Gauge

Gauge is not important in this pattern.

Finished Measurements

8" wide x 8" high (20cm x 20cm)

Materials

2 – (12mm) Animal eyes
(Small parts are a choking hazard)

Tapestry needle

Polyester fiberfill

White strong glue

Stitch marker

Jelly Amigurumi Starfish Pattern

Starfish Leg (make 5 pieces)

- *Work loosely.*

- *Use yarn from outside of the ball, it's straighter and easier to sew the chains when making a foundation chain ring.*

Make a slip knot with a double knot to prevent slipping. Chain 14, straighten, and join with a slip stitch joining the 1st chain. Place marker. Chain 1. Do not turn. (14 ch)

- *Wrap the chain around your finger as you join the chain into the ring, it's easier to see the loops.*

Round 1: Working from right to left, slip stitch loosely into the front loop of each chain around to marker. Do not join.

Round 2: Slip stitch loosely into the front loop of each slip stitch around to marker. Do not join.

Round 3: Repeat Round 2 until leg measures 1¼" (3cm).

- *Move marker to the last stitch made at the end of each round.*

Decrease round: *Insert the hook in the next stitch, yarn over, and pull up a loop, repeat from * once (3 loops on hook), yarn over, and pull through all 3 loops, slip stitch into the front loop of your next stitch and in every stitch around to marker. Do not join. (13 sl st)

Next Round: Repeat Round 2 until leg measures 2" (5cm).

Next Round: Repeat Decrease Round once to marker. (12 sl st)

Next Round: Repeat Round 2 until leg measures 2½" (6cm).

Next Round: Repeat Decrease Round once to marker. (11 sl st)

Next Round: Repeat Round 2 until leg measures 3" (8cm).

Next Round: Repeat Decrease Round once to marker. (10 sl st)

Next Round: Repeat Round 2 until leg measures 3½" (9cm).

Next Round: Repeat Decrease Round once to marker. (9 sl st)

Next Round: Repeat Round 2 until leg measures 4" (10cm).

Next Round: Repeat Decrease Round once to marker. (8 sl st)

Do not fasten off. Cut yarn leaving a 7" (18cm) tail.

Thread tapestry needle with remaining yarn and sew through the top loops of the remaining 8 stitches. Complete last stitch by inserting the yarn tail through the inside of the starfish leg. When finishing and attaching leg to the body, pull the tail end tight from the inside of the leg.

Starfish Body

Front and Back (make 2 pieces)

• *Wrap the chain around your finger as you join the chain into the ring, it's easier to see the loops.*

Make a slip knot with a double knot to prevent slipping.

Loosely chain 6 stitches, straighten, and join with a slip stitch joining the 1st chain. Chain 1. Do not turn. Place marker.

Round 1: 6 single crochet in the center ring and join with a slip stitch to the 1st chain. (6 sc)

Round 2: Make 2 slip stitches in each stitch around to marker. (12 sc)

Repeat Row 2 until the diameter measures 2¼" (6cm).

Last Round: Make 1 slip stitch in each stitch all around.

Fasten off.

Finishing

Assembling Starfish

Fill starfish legs with fiberfill. Use the end of the crochet hook to carefully push fiberfill inside the point of the leg. Gently tighten the opening of the legs.

Holding one leg and the front of the circular body at the same time, whipstitch the outer loops of the body to the 3rd row of front loops of the starfish leg. Repeat for each leg around the circle until all the legs are attached. Thread tapestry needle with 12" (30cm) of yarn and whipstitch the seams closed between the legs.

Turn the starfish over and fill the back of the body with fiberfill. Position the back circular body centered on the back. Whipstitch all around joining the legs with the circular body.

Dip 2 eye shanks in glue and push into front of body. Allow to dry before using.

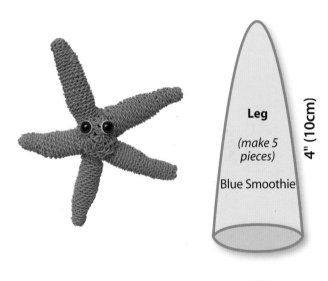

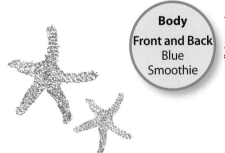

Leg

(make 5 pieces)

Blue Smoothie

4" (10cm)

Body
Front and Back
Blue
Smoothie

1¼" (3cm)

Jellyfish Purse

advanced beginner

Jellyfish are such fun sea creatures! Crochet your very own Jellyfish Purse with Pink Peppermint glow-in-the-dark Jelly Yarn. Recycle an old compact disk to form the circular bottom. Use easy single and double crochet stitches to create this unique design with a drawstring. Fling it over your shoulder for that casual here-I-am look.

Stitch Guide

Chain (ch) page 110

Slip Stitch (sl st) page 111

Single Crochet (sc) page 112

Double Crochet (dc) page 113

Hook

US I/9 (5.5mm) crochet hook.

Yarn

1 ball Fine Jelly Yarn
Color: Pink Peppermint Glow
85yds (78m) / 200g (100% vinyl)

Gauge

14 chain stitches = 4" (10cm)

16 double crochet stitches = 4" (10cm)

4 double crochet rows = 3" (8cm)

Finished Measurements

5" wide x 5" high (12cm x 12cm), not including drawstring straps or curly embellishment

Materials

Compact disk (CD)

Clamp or strong tape

Tapestry needle

Jellyfish Purse Pattern

Bottom

- *The bottom is made by making a long chain and wrapping it around a CD.*

Make a loop with a tight slip knot and place the loop on the hook. Chain 270.

Clamp or tape the 270th chain that is still connected to the yarn ball to the outside edge of the CD with the iridescent side on the outside of the bag. Do not fasten off yarn.

Feed chain strand through center hole of CD and wrap it, without twisting, around the CD from the inner hole to the outer edge to create 20 "chain-spokes" around the CD. Wrap snugly, stretching the chain strand slightly as you go so that each spoke is composed of a total of 13 chains (from rim, through center hole, and

back up to rim again); complete the 20th spoke by ending at the rim and slip stitch to the 270th chain to join. (If you have a few excess chains, ignore them.)

Front or Back

Round 1: With the plain mirror side of the CD facing out (this is the right side or outside of bag), chain 1, single crochet in the joining just made, (chain 2, single crochet in any 2 loops of the chain stitch of the next spoke that is closest to the CD rim) all around, ending with a slip stitch in the 1st single crochet to join. This will form a tight rim around the disk.

Round 2: Chain 1, turn, single crochet in same stitch as joining, (chain 2, single crochet in next single crochet) around, ending with a slip stitch in the 1st single crochet to join. Turn.

Round 3: Chain 2 (counts as 1st double crochet), Double crochet in same stitch as joining, double crochet in each chain and each single crochet around, join round with slip stitch in top of 1st double crochet. Do not turn. (61 dc)

Rounds 4–7: Chain 2 (counts as 1st double crochet), double crochet in back loop only of same double crochet and in back loop only of every double crochet around, join round with a slip stitch in the top of the 1st double crochet. Do not turn.

Round 8: Chain 5 (counts as 1st double crochet and chain 2), skip next 2 double crochet, double crochet in next double crochet, *chain 2, skip next 2 stitches, double crochet in next double crochet, rep from * around, ending with chain 2, slip stitch in 3rd chain of chain-5. Do not turn.

Round 9: Chain 5, (slip stitch in next double crochet, chain 5) around, join with a slip stitch in base of the 1st chain-5.

Fasten off.

Finishing

Jellyfish Tendrils

Leaving a 6" (15cm) yarn tail, make a loop with a slip knot and place the loop on the hook. Chain 12.

Row 1: *2 single crochet in bottom 3rd loop of 2nd chain from hook and bottom 3rd loop of each chain across*. Chain 20, repeat from * to *. Chain 28, repeat from * to *. Fasten off with a 6" (15cm) tail. Stretch each tendril while twisting it for a spiral shape. Tie tendrils to the center of the bag using the yarn tails.

Drawstring Straps (make 2 pieces)

• *Instructions are given for shoulder strap length drawstrings. Length of straps can be made to any desired length; for a handbag, chain 60 or as desired.*

1st Strap

Chain 100. Weave end without twisting through Round 8 of bag so that both ends meet at the outside of the bag; slip stitch in the 1st chain to join drawstring into a ring; slip stitch in the front loop of each chain around; slide drawstring as you go to work into all chains around; slip stitch in 1st slip stitch. Fasten off.

Front Loops

• *Note: For a strap so cool that even crocheters will wonder how you did it, slip stitch into the front loop only of each chain. A chain stitch is made up of 3 loops: 2 top loops that lay somewhat flat, and a third bottom loop that forms a bump. With the two top loops of the chain stitches facing up, work into the one top loop that is closest to you; this is called the "front loop".*

2nd Strap

Make 2nd drawstring same as above. Begin the weaving from the opposite side of the bag without twisting, join as above, and then slip stitch in each chain as above.

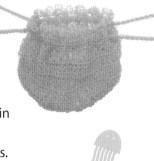

Fasten off. Weave in all ends.

¼" (.63cm)

about 28" (71cm)

Pink Peppermint Glow

Strap

Glows-In-The-Dark!

5" (12cm)

5" (12cm)

Jellyfish Purse

Front or Back
Pink Peppermint Glow

Fun Pack

advanced beginner

The sporty Fun Pack is the perfect carryall for all your cool "stuff". We crocheted it with Blue Smoothie Jelly Yarn using single and double crochet stitches. The handy shoulder strap and chunky zipper make it practical for everyday use. Add a beautiful butterfly appliqué and zipper pull to complete the look.

Stitch Guide

Chain (ch) page 110

Single Crochet (sc) page 112

Double Crochet (dc) page 113

Running stitch page 118

Whipstitch page 118

Hook

US G/6 (4mm) crochet hook, or size needed to obtain gauge.

Yarn

2 balls Fine Jelly Yarn
Color: Blue Smoothie
85yds (78m) / 200g (100% vinyl)

Gauge

16 stitches and 8 rows = 4" (10cm) in double crochet.

Finished Measurements

7½" wide x 6" high (19cm x 15cm)

Materials

7" (18cm) White sport zipper

Tapestry needle

White sewing thread

Sewing needle

Round head pins

Zipper pull clip (optional)

Butterfly appliqué (optional)

Fun Pack Pattern

Front and Back (make 2 pieces)

Chain 33 stitches.

Row 1: Double crochet in 4th chain from hook and in each chain across the row. Chain 3. Turn. (30 dc)

Row 2: Double crochet in each stitch across the row. Chain 3. Turn.

Repeat Row 2 until piece measures 6" (15cm).

Fasten off.

• *Tie a double knot after fastening off with the tail end.*

Gusset

Leave an 18" (46cm) yarn tail for sewing side seams, make a slip knot loop and place on hook. Chain 7 stitches.

Row 1: (Right Side) Double crochet in 4th chain from hook and in each chain across the row. Chain 3. Turn. (5 dc)

Row 2: Double crochet in each stitch across the row. Chain 3. Turn.

Repeat Row 2 until gusset measures 19½" (50cm) or until gusset fits all around left side, bottom, and right side of front piece.

End the row on the Wrong Side.

• *The tail strands should be on opposite corners.*

Fasten off. Leave an 18" (46cm) tail for sewing side seams.

• *Tie a double knot after fastening off.*

Strap

Begin slip knot 8" (20cm) from yarn end, for sewing. Chain 6 stitches.

Row 1: Single crochet in 2nd chain from hook and in every chain across the row. Chain 1. Turn.

Row 2: Single crochet in each stitch across the row. Chain 1.

Repeat Row 2 until strap measures 28" (71cm) or desired length.

End the row with the remaining yarn strand on the Wrong Side. Fasten off

• *The tail strands should be on opposite corners.*

Leave an 18" (46cm) tail for sewing side seams.

• *Tie a double knot after fastening off with the tail end.*

Attach new yarn with a slip stitch at end of any row and loosely slip stitch all around edges of strap working 2 slip stitches into each corner.

Block crochet pieces flat.

Finishing

Sewing Zipper

Place pieces on a flat surface. Place front right side up and align zipper straight along top edge. Pin in position leaving a ¼" (.63cm) gap between the zipper and the top edge of the front piece.

Place back right side up and align zipper straight along top edge. Pin in position leaving a ¼" (.63cm) gap between the zipper and the top edge of the front piece.

Turn wrong side up. Thread the tapestry needle with the remaining yarn strand and sew the zipper to the top edges of the purse using a

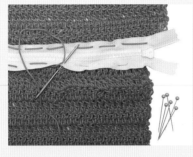

running stitch. Remove the pins as you sew.

- *Make sure needle goes through zipper fabric and crocheting.*

Thread the sewing needle with white thread and whipstitch along the fabric of the zipper, securing it to the crocheting from the wrong side only.

Sewing Front and Gusset

With the front wrong side out, thread the tapestry needle with the remaining yarn tail and sew seams together using a whipstitch. Sew gusset along bottom of bag and up the left side.

Turn bag over with back wrong side out.

- *Open the zipper BEFORE sewing the last side seam.*

Thread the tapestry needle with the remaining yarn tail and sew seams together, using a whipstitch. Sew gusset along bottom of bag and up the right side.

Sewing Shoulder Strap

With zipper closed, thread the tapestry needle with the remaining yarn tail and place the end of the strap 1" (2.5cm) inside the left top side. Using a whipstitch, sew securely. Make sure strap is straight and

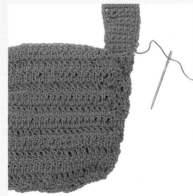

repeat for the other end of right side.

Securing the Zipper

Turn the bag right side out and close the zipper. Thread the tapestry needle with the remaining yarn strand. Tuck zipper ends inside and sew, using a whipstitch stitch, securing them to the shoulder strap.

Attaching Zipper Pull (optional)

Open ring clip and slide it into the hole on the zipper.

Attaching Butterfly Appliqué (optional)

Thread sewing needle with white thread and sew butterfly appliqué to front of purse.

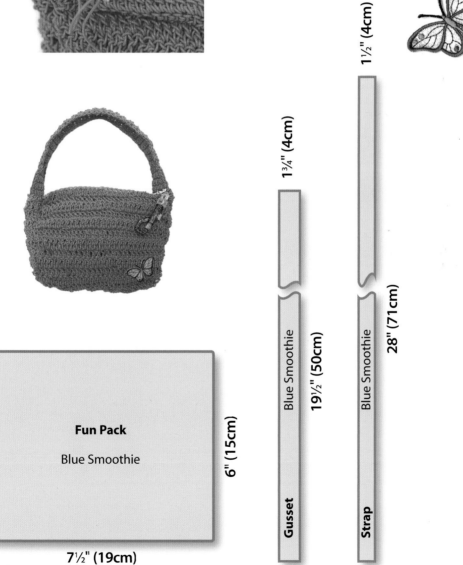

Fun Pack

Blue Smoothie

7½" (19cm)

6" (15cm)

1¾" (4cm)

Blue Smoothie

19½" (50cm)

Gusset

1½" (4cm)

Blue Smoothie

28" (71cm)

Strap

4

How To Knit

Slip Knot

Before you can begin knitting, you will need to learn how to make a slip knot. This is considered the 1st cast on stitch in knitting. After you learn this technique you'll be ready to begin knitting.

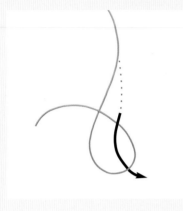

1. *Wind the yarn into a loop.*

2. *Pull the ball yarn through the loop and make a new loop.*

3. *Place the loop on the needle and tighten loosely. You are now ready to cast on stitches and begin knitting.*

Single Cast On (Thumb Cast On)

To begin knitting, you will need to place a number of stitches on the needle as stated in the pattern. The single cast on method is easy to learn, and is ideal for first-time knitters. In a knitting pattern, **CO** is the abbreviation for casting on.

1. *Hold the needle with the slip knot on it in your right hand. Wind the ball yarn clockwise from front to back around your left thumb.*

2. *Slip the needle under the yarn on your left thumb and lift the yarn up off your thumb with the tip of the needle.*

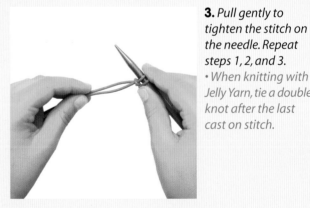

3. *Pull gently to tighten the stitch on the needle. Repeat steps 1, 2, and 3.*
• When knitting with Jelly Yarn, tie a double knot after the last cast on stitch.

Double Cast On (Long Tail Cast On)

The double cast on uses the tail and the ball yarn to cast on stitches to make a sturdy edge. To know where to begin the slip knot, allow 1" (2.5cm) of yarn for each stitch needed, plus 4" (10cm) extra for the tail.

Knit Stitch

Once you cast on the needle, you can begin knitting. The knit stitch is the 1st basic stitch in knitting. In a knitting pattern, **K** is the abbreviation for the knit stitch. Knitting every row creates the **Garter Stitch** pattern.

1. *Wrap the tail yarn around your thumb and the ball yarn around your index finger like a slingshot. Hold the stands in the palm of your hand with your 3 other fingers.*

1. *Insert the tip of the right-hand needle into the 1st cast on stitch from left to right. The tips of the needles form an X, with the right-hand needle below the left-hand needle.*

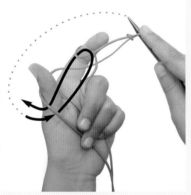

2. *Insert the needle under the yarn on your thumb from the front to the back and lift. Then, insert the needle behind the yarn on your index finger, and back through the loop on your thumb lifting the yarn from back to front.*

2. *Wind the ball yarn counterclockwise from back to front around the tip of the right-hand needle. Slide the tip of the right-hand needle up through the stitch and lift it onto the right-hand needle.*

3. *Slide loops off your fingers onto the needle and tighten gently. Repeat steps 1, 2, and 3 until all the stitches are cast on the needle.*
• When knitting with Jelly Yarn, tie a double knot with the ball and yarn strands after the last cast on stitch.

3. *As you complete each stitch, slide the remaining stitches up to the tip of the needle. Repeat steps 1, 2, and 3 until all stitches are on the right-hand needle. When making a knit stitch, make sure the yarn is always* ***behind*** *the needles.*

Knit Through the Back Loop

Knitting through the back loop creates a twisted stitch that is ideal for Jelly Yarn. The result is a stitch pattern that is less bumpy, and has a flat texture.

I-Cord

The I-cord looks like a difficult stitch, but is simple to learn using double-pointed needles. You can make an I-cord using 3 to 5 stitches. We used the 3 stitch I-cord to make the Fun Belt, Jump Rope, and Bracelets.

1. *Insert the tip of the right-hand needle into the back of the loop on the left-hand needle, from right to left.*

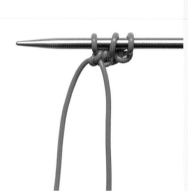

1. *Cast on 3 stitches on double-pointed needles.*

2. *Wind the ball yarn counterclockwise from back to front around the tip of the right-hand needle.*

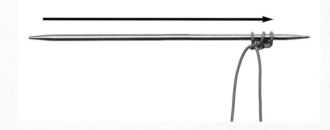

2. *Without turning the needle, slide the stitches to the right point.*

3. *Slide the tip of the right-hand needle up through the stitch and lift it up onto the right-hand needle. Repeat steps 1, 2, and 3 as needed.*

3. *Knit the 3 stitches across the row. It's important to pull **tightly** after the 1st knit stitch. Repeat steps 2, and 3 for desired length.*

Purl Stitch

The Purl stitch is the second basic stitch in knitting. When purling, remember to keep the ball of yarn in front of the needles. In a knitting pattern, **P** is the abbreviation for the purl stitch. Knit 1 stitch, purl 1 stitch across, creates the **Stockinette Stitch** pattern.

Slip a Stitch Purlwise

Some patterns indicate slipping the 1st stitch purlwise, for a clean, even edge. This method creates a chain selvedge edge. We slipped the 1st stitch purlwise to make the Pet Collar and Mini Purse projects.

1. *With the yarn in front of the needles, insert the tip of the right-hand needle into the front of the 1st stitch, from right to left.*

1. *Bring the yarn in **front** as if to purl.*

2. *Wrap the yarn counterclockwise from back to front around the tip of the right-hand needle.*
• Remember, when making a purl stitch always keep the yarn in front of the needles.

2. *Insert the needle from right to left, as if to purl.*

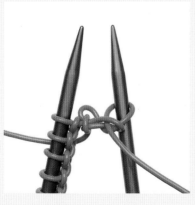

3. *Slide the right-hand needle back through the stitch and slip the original stitch off the left-hand needle. As you complete each stitch, slide the remaining stitches up to the tip of the needle. Repeat steps 1, 2, and 3 until all the stitches are on the right-hand needle.*

3. *Slip the 1st stitch purlwise onto the right-hand needle. Bring the yarn back, and work the remaining stitches across the row as directed in the pattern.*

Knitting In The Round

Use circular needles to knit in the round. Stitches are cast on, then joined. Place a marker at the join to show you when the round begins. The Beach Bag project uses circular needles.

Bind Off

To complete your project, you'll need to bind off. This method prevents the stitches from unraveling, and creates an even, finished edge. In a knitting pattern, **BO** is the abbreviation for binding off.

first cast on stitch   last cast on stitch

1. *Begin with the right needle and cast on desired number of stitches or as instructed in the pattern. Place on a flat surface and straighten all the stitches facing inside the circle.*

1. *Knit the 1st 2 stitches.*

2. *Place the right-hand needle with the last stitch made, into the 1st stitch cast on the left-hand needle. Join these stitches together with a knit stitch or knit the two stitches together. Pull tightly so there is no gap.*

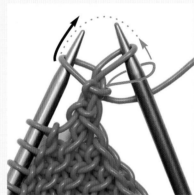

2. *With the left-hand needle, lift the 1st stitch up over the second stitch, and completely off the right-hand needle.*

3. *Place a stitch marker on the right needle. As you knit, make sure the join stays closed. Slide your stitches as you knit, with each round. When you reach the marker slide it to the right needle, counting each new round.*

3. *Knit the next stitch, and repeat step 2 until one stitch remains on the left-hand needle. Lift the final stitch off the needle and cut the yarn leaving a 6" (15cm) tail. Make a tight double knot.*

Changing Yarns and Weaving Ends

You will need to change yarns in projects with more than 1 ball or color of yarn. Change yarn at the end of a row to make it easier to weave in the loose ends when you are finished.

1. *Make a slip knot with the new yarn and pull the old yarn through. Cut old yarn, leaving a 6" (15cm) tail.*

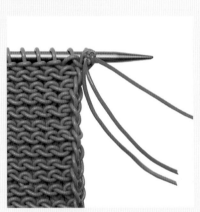

2. *Slide the slip knot up to the needle. Tie a tight double knot with the old and new yarn tails. Continue knitting across the row as instructed in the pattern.*

3. *To weave ends, thread a tapestry needle with the tail. Working on the wrong side, insert the needle under 5–6 top loops and pull through to weave the yarn. Tie a tight, double knot in the last loop. Careful the piece doesn't curl when pulling the knot.*

• *This sample shows contrasting colors for visibility. Always weave the same colors on the same side.*

Knitting Pattern Basics

Although we did not use abbreviations in this book, knitting patterns are written with abbreviations to save space. Now you are ready to learn how to read a knitting pattern. Remember to always read all instructions completely before beginning to knit the pattern.

Skill Levels

Beginner Projects for first-time knitters, using knit stitch, with minimal sewing.

Easy Projects using knit stitch with some assembly.

Advanced Beginner Projects using knit and/or purl stitches, with assembly.

Yarn Label Information

Information on the ball band provides the length, weight, material content, and yarn color:

Jelly Yarn – Bulky 65 yards per ball, 60 meters per ball, 240 grams per ball, material content 100% Vinyl, yarn color Blue Taffy.

Gauge and Tension

Most projects in this book do not require a specific gauge. However, there are a few projects where gauge is important. Gauge is the number of stitches and rows over a standard measure, usually 4" (10cm). Before knitting a pattern, knit a 4" (10cm) practice swatch using the needles recommended in the pattern. Check your swatch against the gauge in the pattern. Tension refers to how tight or how loose your stitches are on the needle. If the number of stitches is greater than the gauge, your stitches are too small, switch to larger needles. If the number of stitches is fewer than the gauge, your stitches are too big, switch to smaller needles.

• This is an example of gauge:
12 stitches and 8 rows = 4" (10cm)

Needles

Knitting needles are available in different sizes. We recommend using metal needles with Jelly Yarn. Every pattern lists a needle size for that pattern. If the recommended needle size does not match your gauge, change needles. Larger needles produce fewer stitches, and smaller needles produce more stitches.

• This is an example of needle size:
US 8 (5mm) needles, or size needed to obtain gauge.

5

How To Crochet

Slip Knot

Before you can begin crocheting, you will need to learn how to make a slip knot. The slip knot is not considered a chain. After you make a slip knot, you will be ready to start crocheting!

Chain Stitch and Foundation Row

The chain stitch forms the foundation row in crochet. This stitch is like casting on in knitting. The yarn over is the basic step used to create chain stitches. In crochet patterns, ch and yo are the abbreviations for chain stitch and yarn over.

1. *Wind the yarn into a loop.*

1. *Make the 1st chain stitch by wrapping the yarn around the hook from the back to the front. This is called a yarn over.*

2. *Pull the ball yarn through the loop and make a new loop.*

2. *Pull the hook through the loop to make the 1st chain.*

3. *Place the loop on the crochet hook and tighten loosely. You are now ready to make your chain.*

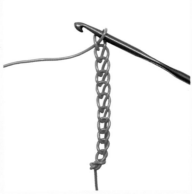

3. *Repeat steps 1 and 2 by making another yarn over and drawing the hook through the loop. Continue making several chain stitches until you can make the stitches uniform and even. Practice makes perfect!*

Slip Stitch

The stitch is used to join yarns, create a firm edge, or introduce new colors. A slip stitch also makes a chain thicker. In a crochet pattern, **sl st** is the abbreviation for the slip stitch.

Crocheting a Center Ring

Crocheting a center ring is your foundation for working in rounds. To create a center ring, make a foundation chain and join the ends with a slip stitch to join the ring. This technique is used to make the Snow Globe Flower and the Amigurumi Starfish.

1. *Insert the hook into the second chain from the hook, or the stitch indicated in the pattern. Yarn over by wrapping the yarn around the hook from the back to the front.*

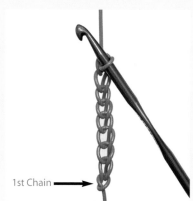
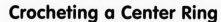

1st Chain ➡

1. *Chain the number of stitches needed.*

2. *Pull the hook through the chain or stitch.*

2. *Insert the hook into the 1st chain stitch and yarn over.*
• To help see the stitches, you can wrap the chain around your finger.

3. *Then, pull through the next loop on the hook. (1 loop remains on the hook)*

3. *Pull the hook through the chain and the loop on the hook. (1 slip stitch completed)*

Single Crochet Around a Ring

Single crochet around a ring adds a decorative support and creates the stitches to work in rounds. This technique is used to make the Flying Jelly Ring, Tamborine, Sports Bottle Sling, and Jelly Bracelets.

Single Crochet

The single crochet stitch is a basic compact stitch. If the 1st stitch of a row or round is a single crochet, chain one at the end of the previous row or round to get to the correct height. In a crochet pattern, **sc** is the abbreviation for the single crochet stitch.

1. *Make a slip knot and place on hook. With yarn under hook, place hook into ring and yarn over.*

1. *Insert the hook into the second chain from the hook or stitch indicated, and yarn over by wrapping the yarn around the hook from the back to the front.*

2. *Slide the hook over the top of the ring and yarn over.*

2. *Pull up a loop through the chain or stitch. (2 loops remain on the hook)*

3. *Pull yarn through 2 loops. (1 single crochet) Repeat steps 1, 2, and 3 working around ring. When complete, join 1st and last single crochet stitches with a slip stitch.*

3. *Yarn over and pull the hook through 2 loops. (1 loop remains on the hook) Repeat steps 1, 2, and 3 as needed.*

Double Crochet

A double crochet stitch is three times as high as a single crochet stitch. If the 1st stitch of a row or round is a double crochet, you usually chain three at the end of the previous row or round to reach the correct height.

In a crochet pattern, **dc** is the abbreviation for a double crochet stitch. Double crochet is used to make the Jelly Boot Sleeves, Jellyfish Purse, and the Fun Pack.

1. *Yarn over, insert the hook into the fourth chain from the hook or the stitch indicated.*

4. *Yarn over.*

2. *Yarn over.*

5. *Pull the hook through the 1st 2 loops. (2 loops remain on the hook)*

3. *Pull up a loop through the chain or stitch. [The 1st three chains at the beginning count as a double crochet.] (3 loops remain on the hook)*

6. *Yarn over and pull the hook through the last 2 loops. (1 loop remains on the hook) Repeat steps 1–6 as needed. (1 double crochet completed)*

Decrease 2 Single Crochet

This single crochet decrease works two stitches together to shape your project. In a crochet pattern, **sc2tog** is the abbreviation for decrease 2 single crochet stitch. Decrease 2 single crochet is used in the Amigurumi Starfish project.

Changing Yarns and Weaving Ends

You will need to change yarns in projects with more than 1 ball or color of yarn. Change yarn at the end of a row to make it easier to weave in the loose ends when you are finished. In the Fun Pack, change yarns to join a 2nd ball of yarn.

1. Insert the hook into the next stitch, yarn over, and pull up a loop. (2 loops on hook)

1. Double crochet to the last stitch leaving 2 loops on the hook. Drop the old yarn and hook the new yarn.

2. Insert the hook into the next stitch, yarn over, and pull up a loop. (3 loops on hook)

2. Pull up a loop with the new yarn through the 2 loops. (1 double crochet completed) Make a double knot with the old and new yarn strands. Continue crocheting as instructed in the pattern.

3. Yarn over and pull through all 3 loops.

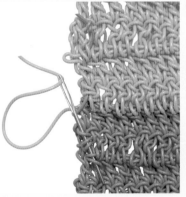

3. To weave ends, thread a tapestry needle with the tail. Working on the wrong side, insert the needle under the post loops. Tie a tight, double knot in the last loop. Careful the piece doesn't curl when pulling the knot. Repeat for each remaining tail.

• This sample shows contrasting colors for visibility. Always weave the same colors on the same side.

Fastening Off

As you complete crocheting each section, you will need to secure the end of your crocheting. This technique prevents unraveling your project. This is called fastening off.

1. *Begin fastening off by cutting a 6" (15cm) as instructed in the pattern from the completed project.*

2. *Yarn over using the tail strand.*

3. *Draw the tail through the last remaining loop and pull gently to tighten. Then, make a tight double knot through the loop.*

Crochet Pattern Basics

Although we did not use abbreviations in this book, crochet patterns are written with abbreviations to save space. Now you are ready to learn how to read a crochet pattern. Remember to always read all instructions completely before beginning to crochet the pattern.

Skill Levels

Beginner Projects for first-time crocheters, using slip stitch and/or single crochet, with minimal sewing.

Easy Projects using slip stitch, single crochet, double crochet, and/or crocheting around a ring, with some assembly.

Advanced Beginner Projects using slip stitch, single crochet, double crochet, decrease, and/or crocheting in the round, with assembly.

Yarn Label Information

Information on the ball band provides the length, weight, material content, and yarn color:

Jelly Yarn – Fine 85 yards per ball, 78 meters per ball, 200 grams per ball, material content 100% Vinyl, yarn color Lemon-Lime Ice.

Gauge and Tension

Most projects in this book do not require a specific gauge. However, there are a few projects where gauge is important. Gauge is the number of stitches and rows over a standard measure, usually 4" (10cm). Before crocheting a pattern, make a 4" (10cm) practice swatch using the hook recommended in the pattern. Check your swatch against the gauge in the pattern. Tension refers to how tight or how loose you made your stitches. If the number of stitches is greater than the gauge, your stitches are too small and switch to a larger hook. If the number of stitches is fewer than the gauge, your stitches are too big, switch to a smaller hook.

• This is an example of gauge:
20 stitches (sts) and 10 rows = 4" (10cm)

Hooks

Crochet hooks are available in different sizes. We recommend using metal hooks with Jelly Yarn. Every pattern lists a hook size for that pattern. If the recommended hook size does not match your gauge, change hooks. Larger hooks produce fewer stitches, and smaller hooks produce more stitches.

• This is an example of hook size:
US K/10.5 (6.5mm) crochet hook, or size needed to obtain gauge.

6

Important Stuff

Whipstitch

For some patterns, you need to sew the pieces together. The whipstitch is a strong stitch for assembling your knit or crochet projects, as well as sewing buckles, rings, and purse straps. This technique works well on any stitch pattern.

Running Stitch

The running stitch or straight stitch is a simple, basic stitch that is often used as a foundation for more complex stitches. This stitch is used to sew the Beach Bag drawstring and the Fun Pack zipper.

1. Buckles
Thread a tapestry needle with Jelly Yarn. Line up the edge and buckle bar. Wrap the yarn up and over the edge and insert the needle back into the edge. Repeat evenly on both sides of the tine joining the buckle and edge together.

Tine

1. *For the Fun Pack, place the zipper in position with the right sides facing and pin in position.*

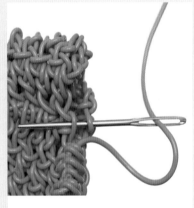

2. Knitting or Crocheting
Thread a tapestry needle with Jelly Yarn. Align the two pieces evenly and pin together with the right sides facing. Insert the needle from back to front 2 times to secure the corners, then wrap the yarn up and over the seams. Repeat using the whipstitch along the edges to join the side seams together.

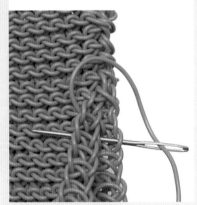

For Knit through the Back Loop seams, insert the needle through the 2 loops on each edge.

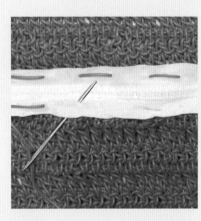

2. *Thread a tapestry needle with Jelly Yarn. Pass the needle in and out of the fabric in a straight line, making all the stitches of equal length.*
• *Use this technique for sewing the Beach Bag drawstring.*

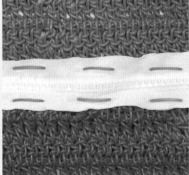

3. *Repeat steps 2 and 3, or as indicated in the pattern. When completed, tie a double knot.*

Knitting Needles & Crochet Hooks

Knit US and UK Needle Sizes

US Sizes	Millimeter Sizes	UK Sizes
0	2.00 mm	14
1	2.25 mm	13
2	2.75 mm	12
-	3.00 mm	11
3	3.25 mm	10
4	3.50 mm	-
5	3.75 mm	9
6	4.00 mm	8
7	4.50 mm	7
8	5.00 mm	6
9	5.50 mm	5
10	6.00 mm	4
10½	6.50 mm	3
-	7.00 mm	2
-	7.50 mm	1
11	8.00 mm	0
13	9.00 mm	00
15	10.00 mm	000
17	12.00 mm	-
19	16.00 mm	-
35	19.00 mm	-
50	25.00 mm	-

Crochet US and UK Hook Sizes

US Sizes	Millimeter Sizes	UK Sizes
B-1	2.25 mm	12
C-2	2.75 mm	11
D-3	3.25 mm	10
E-4	3.50 mm	9
F-5	3.75 mm	8
G-6	4.00 mm	7
7	4.50 mm	-
H-8	5.00 mm	6
I-9	5.50 mm	5
J-10	6.00 mm	4
K-10½	6.50 mm	3
L-11	8.00 mm	-
M/N-13	9.00 mm	-
N/P-15	10.00 mm	-
P/Q	15.00 mm	-
Q	16.00 mm	-
S	19.00 mm	-

Knit US and UK Terminology

US	UK
bind off	cast off
gauge	tension
right side	right front
skip a stitch	miss a stitch
Stockinette Stitch	Stocking Stitch

Crochet US and UK Terminology

US	UK
ch – chain	ch – chain
sl st – slip stitch	ss – slip stitch
sc – single crochet	dc – double crochet
dc – double crochet	tr – treble
hdc – half double crochet	htr – half treble
tr – treble	dtr – double treble
dtr – double treble	trtr – triple treble
yo – yarn over hook	yoh – yarn over hook
fasten off	cast off
skip	miss
gauge	tension
work even	work straight

Skill Level Guide

Knit Projects

Beginner
Projects for first-time knitters, using the knit stitch, I-cord, or knit through the back loop, with minimal sewing.

Jelly Jewelry page16

Glow Diary Cover page 20

Pet Collar and Leash page 24

Easy
Projects using the knit stitch, I-cord, or knit through the back loop, with some assembly.

Jump Rope page 28

Fun Belt page 32

Feather Party Purse page 36

Jewelry Box page 40

Mini Purse page 44

Advanced Beginner
Projects using the knit and/or purl stitches, knit through the back loop, or circular knitting with some assembly.

Beach Bag page 48

Knapsack page 52

Crochet Projects

Beginner
Projects for first-time crocheters, using the slip stitch and/or single crochet, with minimal sewing.

Glow Belt page 58

Flying Jelly Ring page 62

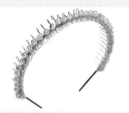
Hair Accessories page 66

Easy
Projects using the slip stitch, single crochet, double crochet, and/or crochet around a ring with some assembly.

Jelly Boot Sleeves page 70

Sports Bottle Sling page 74

Jelly Bracelets 78

Snow Globe Flower page 82

Jelly Amigurumi Starfish page 86

Advanced Beginner
Projects using the slip stitch, single crochet, double crochet, decrease and/or crochet in the round with assembly.

Jellyfish Purse page 90

Fun Pack page 94

Stitch Patterns

**I-Cord Stitch
Knit Projects**

**Garter Stitch
Knit Projects**

**Knit Through the
Back Loop Stitch
Knit Projects**

Jelly Jewelry page 16

*Feather Party Purse
page 36*

Glow Diary Cover page 20

Jump Rope page 28

*Pet Collar and Leash
page 24*

**Stockinette Stitch
Knit Projects**

Jewelry Box page 40

Fun Belt page 32

Knapsack page 52

Mini Purse page 44

Beach Bag page 48

Slip Stitch Crochet Projects

Single Crochet Projects

Double Crochet Projects

Flying Jelly Ring page 62

Glow Belt page 58

Jelly Boot Sleeves page 70

Hair Accessories page 66

Jelly Bracelets 78

Snow Globe Flower page 82

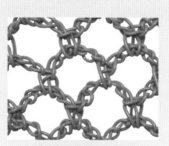

Chain-5 Crochet Project

Jellyfish Purse page 90

Jelly Amigurumi Starfish page 86

Sports Bottle Sling page 74

Fun Pack page 94

About the Authors

Kathleen Greco and Nick Greco

Authors Kathleen and Nick Greco of Dimensional Illustrators, Inc. have been designing and publishing craft books since 1989. As illustrated book packagers, the Grecos are both actively involved in all aspects of the book packaging industry including concept development, research, design, editing, photography, and production. An experienced knitting and crochet designer, Kathleen's creations are featured in trade magazines, books, and specialty boutiques. Nick responsibilities include copywriting, editing all published material, and coordinating the packaged book from initial purchase order to final bound copy.

Kathleen is credited with the innovation and development of Jelly Yarn®. This cool retro-techno yarn, specially created for knitting and crochet, is featured in magazine and specialty knitting and crochet publications worldwide. Kathleen's design patterns and Jelly Yarns are available at: www.jellyyarns.com. The Grecos live and work in beautiful Bucks County, Pennsylvania.

Jelly Yarn Resources

Online Retail Sales

www.jellyyarns.com

Jelly Yarn is available at yarn shops, craft chains, and at these select retail stores worldwide:

United States

California
Michael Levine, Inc.
919 South Maple Ave.
Los Angeles, CA 90015
213.689.1363

Alabama
The Taming of the Ewe
26 Public Square
Jacksonville, AL 36265
256.782.9080

Michigan
Knit A Round
2663 Plymouth Road
Traver Village Shopping Center
Ann Arbor, MI 48105
734.998.3771

Mississippi
Yarn Basket
705B South Main St.
Petal, MS 39465
601.582.7272

Ohio
Royalwood Ltd.
517 Woodville Rd.
Mansfield, Ohio 44907
419.526.1630
800.526.1630 (toll free)

Pennsylvania
Knit Together
Mallard Creek Shopping Ctr.
130 Almshouse Rd/Ste 206
Richboro, PA 18954
215.355.3531

Virginia
Crafts & Things
385 Valley Street
Scottsdale, VA 24590
434.286.2396

United Kingdom
I Knit
106 Lower Marsh
Waterloo, London UK
SE1 7AB
020.7261.1338
www.iknit.org.uk

Contributing Designers

Vashti Braha
Flying Jelly Ring • Sports Bottle Sling • Jellyfish Purse

Vashti Braha currently serves on the board of directors of the Crochet Guild of America. Her designs, whether kooky or serious fashion, can be found in various books, magazines, and CGOA's own Pattern Line (www.crochet.org). When she's not exploring the unlimited potential of crochet, she helps her young son design his own quirky toys. Vashti teaches "Trendy Crochet" nationally, and maintains an informative creative blog at www.designingvashti.blogspot.com.

Judy Patkos
Jump Rope

Judy Patkos is a knitting teacher and knitwear designer. Her specialty is Fair Isle knitting. Judy applied her knowledge of color stranding to the unique two-color Jelly Yarn Jump Rope pattern. A yarn color enthusiast, she has her own line of hand dyed wool yarns aptly named Jujuknits. Judy serves as the vice president of the Bucks County Knit and Crochet Guild, in Pennsylvania.

Carrie A. Sullivan
Hair Accessories • Jelly Boot Sleeves Idea

Carrie A. Sullivan is a passionate crochet teacher and handbag designer. Her current book, *Carry Alongs: 15 Crochet Handbags & Purses for Every Occasion* (Krause Publications), showcases contemporary purse and handbag designs for the stylish crocheter. Carrie's designs are featured in crochet magazines and books including Knit 1 and The Knitter's Guide to Combining Yarns. She is the secretary of the Bucks County Knit and Crochet Guild, in Pennsylvania.

Fashion Photographer

Joe VanDeHatert
Joe VanDeHatert of Studio V, is a noted Cincinnati-based advertising and fashion photographer. His work is featured in many knit and crochet books including *Carry Alongs: 15 Crochet Handbags & Purses for Every Occasion* (Krause Publications). Joe's portfolio is available at: www.studiovcincy.com.

Partial Wardrobe Contributor

Mimi & Maggie
Mimi & Maggie's product range is for girls, starting from infants, 12M to approximately age 12, that includes jeans, tops, skirts, sweaters, coats and dresses. They find inspiration in the individuality of children and their art and honor their free spirits, joy of discovery and happiness in the simple pleasures of life. Mimi & Maggie strive to blend the handicrafts of world cultures, incorporating the beauty and craftsmanship into modern day garments.

Mimi & Maggie
1425 S. Grande Vista Avenue
Los Angeles, CA 90023
323.264.0200
info@mimiandmaggie.com
www.mimiandmaggie.com

Material Resources

Needles, notions, snaps and thread are not listed, they are available at craft or sewing stores. (Warning: Small parts are a choking hazard)

16 Jelly Jewelry

Jewelry clasps / *Metal Maddness*

½" (1cm) and ¾" (2cm) Jump rings (necklace) / *Jewelry Essentials™*

Star and butterfly charms with ring (bracelet) / *Jewelry Essentials™*

Heart and shoe charms with ring (bracelet) / *Jewelry Essentials™*

Round pendant (necklace) / *Darice®*

Mini chain nose pliers / *Jewelry Essentials™*

20 Glow Diary Cover

Spiral notebook / any 5" high x 7" wide (13cm x 18cm) / *any brand*

(5mm) Glow-in-the-dark pony beads / *Westrim Crafts®*

Alphabet beads / *Jewelry Essentials™*

Key charms / *Jewelry Essentials™*

Strong white glue / *any brand*

24 Pet Collar and Leash

¾" (2cm) Buckle / *Dritz®*

Swivel clips / *Dritz®*

32 Fun Belt

Belt buckle 1½" (4cm) opening / *Dritz®*

36 Feather Party Purse

Pink feather boa / *Zucker Feather Products*

40 Jewelry Box

Rhinestone crystals / *Darice®*

44 Mini Purse

Decorative button / *Dress It Up®*

48 Beach Bag

Cord stop / *Dritz®*

58 Glow Belt

1¼" (3cm) Belt buckle / *www.jellyyarns.com*

62 Flying Jelly Ring

9½" (24cm) diameter round plastic canvas / *any brand*

8" (20cm) x 10" (25cm) Red, Yellow, Blue self-stick felt or foam sheets / *any brand*

5" (12cm) diameter metal craft ring (Tambourine) / *any brand*

10 Large metal jingle bells / *Darice®*

66 Hair Accessories

2½" (6cm) Automatic clasp barrette / *Scünci*

3" (8cm) Oval clip barrettes / *Scünci*

(7mm) Round glass beads, mixed colors / *Jewelry Essentials™*

Comb headband with 37 teeth / *Scünci*

(7mm) Pink round glass beads / *Jewelry Essentials™*

70 Jelly Boot Sleeves

Flower buttons / *www.jellyyarns.com*

Pair of rubber rain boots (kids' size) / *JoAnn Fabric*

74 Sport Bottle Sling

1" (2.5cm) Blue plastic rings / *Linked™*

78 Jelly Bracelets

1" (2.5cm) Rings (blue, red) / *Linked™*

½" (1cm) Green bangle bracelet / *Claire's®*

82 Snow Globe Flower

3" (8cm) Snow globe kit / *www.jellyyarns.com*

Plastic Model glue / *any brand*

Ear syringe / *any brand*

86 Jelly Amigurumi Starfish

(12mm) Animal eyes / *Darice®*

Polyester fiberfill / *any brand*

White strong glue / *any brand*

90 Jellyfish Purse

4½" (11cm) diameter Compact disk (CD) / *any brand*

Clamp or strong tape / *any brand*

94 Fun Pack

7" (18cm) White sport zipper / *Coats & Clark*

Zipper pull clip / *Darice®*

Butterfly appliqué / *JoAnn Fabrics*

Abbreviations

To make the patterns in this book kid-friendly, we have eliminated the use of abbreviations; however, most knitting and crochet patterns use them to save space. Below is a list of common knitting and crochet abbreviations.

Knit Abbreviations

BO – bind off
cm – centimeter(s)
CO – cast on
g – gram
Garter st – knit every row
In or " – inch(es)
K – knit
K2tog – knit 2 stitches together
m – meter
mm – millimeter
P – purl
patt – pattern
pm – place stitch marker

rep – repeat
rep from * – repeat pattern
   after *
rnd(s) – round(s)
RS – right side
Sl 1 P – slip 1 stitch purlwise
sl st – slip stitch
st(s) – stitch(es)
St st – Stockinette stitch
   (knit 1 row, purl 1 row; repeat)
tog – together
WS – wrong side
yd(s) – yard(s)

Crochet Abbreviations

beg – begin
ch – chain stitch
cm – centimeter(s)
dc – double crochet
g – gram
lp(s) – loops
m – meter
mm – millimeter(s)
patt – pattern
pm – place marker
rep – repeat
rep from * – repeat pattern
   after *

rnd(s) – round(s)
RS – right side
sc – single crochet
sl st – slip stitch
st(s) – stitch(es)
tog – together
WS – wrong side
yd(s) – yard(s)
yo – yarn over

Index